THE CATHOLIC HYMNAL

Hymns for Liturgical Celebration
English Edition
with the
Order of the Mass and Masses
from the Kyriale

AN OSV PASTORAL PUBLICATION

Nihil Obstat: LAWRENCE A. GOLLNER
Censor Librorum
Imprimatur: ✠ LEO A. PURSLEY
Bishop of Fort Wayne-South Bend
January 25, 1974

ISBN: 0-87973-781-6
Library of Congress Catalogue Card Number: 73-93534

Acknowledgements:

Acknowledgement is made to the large number of people who generously gave their time to discussing and selecting the hymns used in this book. Complete information is given on the respective pages on which each song appears. If any copyright has been unwittingly misstated or infringed, the publisher offers apologies and will rectify the omission in the next printing. The compiler is grateful to all who made their material available for use in this hymnal: The American Catholic Press, Oak Park, Ill.; Capuchin Troupe, St. Louis, Mo.; E. J. Dwyer Pty. Ltd. (Australia); Sister Claudia Foltz, Marylhurst, Oregon; Franciscan Communications Center, Los Angeles, Calif.; Gregorian Institute of America, Chicago, Ill.; Monsignor Martin B. Hellriegel, St. Louis, Mo.; Jan-Lee Music, Beverley Hills, Calif.; Lexicon Music, Inc., Woodland Hills, Calif.; Moody Bible Institute, Chicago, Ill.; Rev. A. Nigro, S.J., Spokane, Wash.; The Rodeheaver Co., Winona Lake, Ind.; A. P. Schmidt Co., Chicago, Ill.; Singspiration, Inc., Grand Rapids, Mich.; Word Music, Inc., Waco, Texas; David Yantis; and the many authors whose works are credited with their hymns.

Cover design by James E. McIlrath

Printed and bound in the United States of America by Our Sunday Visitor, Inc., Huntington, Indiana, 46750.

781

Alphabetical Contents

CONTENTS

The Order of the Mass	pages 23 thru 33
	No.
Abide with Me	189
A Child's Prayer	183
A Mighty Fortress Is Our God	88
Agnus Dei — (de Angelis)	236
Agnus Dei — (Orbis Factor)	231
Alas! And Did My Savior Bleed?	188
Alleluia 1 (Palestrina)	133
Alleluia 2 (Chant)	134
Alleluia 3 (Chant)	135
Alleluia 4 (Byzantine)	136
Alleluia 5	137
Alleluia	138
Alleluia / Praise to You (same Melody)	140a
All Glory, Laud, and Honor	30
All Hail the Power of Jesus' Name	21
All People That on Earth Do Dwell	191
All the Ends of the Earth	7
All Things Through Christ	89
Amazing Grace!	90
Amen (Spiritual)	91
Amen 1	154
Amen 2	155
Amen (Danish)	156
Amen (Dresden)	157
America	123
America, the Beautiful	122
Angels, from the Realms of Glory	190
Angels We Have Heard on High	8
Art Thou Weary?	195
As the Dewy Shades of Even	198
As with Gladness Men of Old	18
At the Cross Her Station Keeping	33
At the Lamb's High Feast	37
Away in the Manger	194

Ballad of the Passion 32
Battle Hymn of the Republic 124
Behold the Living Bread 55
Be Joyful, Mary 39
Beyond a Dream 125
Blessed Is He 93
Breathe on Me, Breath of God 46
Bring Back the Springtime 94
Bringing in the Sheaves 95
Bringing Myrrh, Gold and Incense 19

Canticle of the Gift 80
Christ Has Died 1 148
Christ Has Died 2 149
Christ the Lord Is Ris'n Today 38
Christians, Let Us Love One Another 81
Come as a Child 96
Come, Holy Ghost 47
Come, Thou Long Expected Jesus 1
Communion Song 82
Credo III 229
Crown Him with Many Crowns 57

Danish Amen 156
Dear Saint Joseph 181
Deo Gratias (de Angelis) 237
Deo Gratias (Orbis Factor) 232
Doxology after the Lord's Prayer 160, 161
Dresden Amen 157
Dying You Destroyed Our Death 150

Faith of Our Fathers 68
Fill My Cup, Lord 97
Follow Me 98
For All the Blessings 99
For the Kingdom . . . 1 160
For the Kingdom . . . 2 161

Gentle Like You 22
Gloria (de Angelis) 234
Gloria (Orbis Factor) 228
Glorious God 59
Glory to God in the Highest 1 130
Glory to God in the Highest 2 131
Glory to God in the Highest 3 132

God and Man at Table Are Sat Down 87
God Bless Our Native Land 222
God Father, Praise and Glory 51
God Gives Us an Angel 179
Go Down, Moses 200
Go Now and Live for the Savior 100
Go, Tell It on the Mountain 9
Going Home Song 182
Good King Wenceslas 193
Grafted on the Vine 101
Great Is the Lord 60

Hail, Holy Queen 71
Hail Mary 70
Hark, Hark, My Soul 226
Hark, the Herald Angels Sing 11
Have Mercy on Me 29
Heart of Mary 202
Heart Speaks to Heart 102
He Leadeth Me 203
He Lives 41
Holy God, We Praise Thy Name 61
Holy, Holy, Holy 1 145
Holy, Holy, Holy 2 146
Holy, Holy, Holy 3 147
Holy, Holy, Holy! Lord God Almighty 52
Holy Patron 205
How Lovely Is Your Dwelling Place (Ps. 84) 84
Humbly Let Us Voice Our Homage 167
Hymn for Renewal 103
Hymn of the Angels 206
Hymn to the Pope 207

I Am the Bread of Life 85
I Need Thee Every Hour 204
I Saw the New Jerusalem 104
I'm So Glad 169
Immaculate Mary 72
Indian Magnificat 73
In Praise of God 171
In the Beginning Was the Word 2
In the Fullness of Time 3

Jesus Christ Is Ris'n Today 42
Jesus, Love Is in Your Heart 172

Jesus, Lover of My Soul 209
Jesus Loves Me, This I Know 220
Jesus, My Lord, My God 213
Jesus, on the Cross You Died 173
Jesus Shall Reign 40
Jesus the Only Thought of Thee 23
Joyful, Joyful, We Adore Thee 105
Joy to the World! 10

Kyrie (de Angelis) 233
Kyrie (Orbis Factor) 227

Lamb of God 1 162
Lamb of God 2 163
Lamb of God 3 164
Lamb of God 4 165
Lead, Kindly Light 212
Learn of Me 56
Let All That Is Within Me Cry Holy 106
Let There Be Peace on Earth 107
Like a Lamb Who Needs the Shepherd 108
Lord, By Your Cross and Resurrection 152
Lord, Dismiss Us 92
Lord God of Morning 196
Lord, Have Mercy 1 127
Lord, Have Mercy 2 128
Lord, Have Mercy 3 129
Lord Who Throughout These Forty Days 27

Maranatha 4
Mary, My Mother 180
Mary's Joy 74
Mother of the Americas 75
My God, How Wonderful 192

Nearer My God to Thee 210
Nobody Knows the Trouble I've Seen 201
Now Thank We All Our God 62
Now the Day Is Over 197

O Come, All Ye Faithful 13
O Come, O Come, Emmanuel 5
O Little Town of Bethlehem 12
O Lord, We Bless You 63
O Purest of Creatures 199

O Queen of Heaven 43
O Sacred Head 34
O Saving Victim 166
O Virgin Most Wise 77
O Workman Worthy 79
On Jordan's Bank 6
Only a Veil 24
On This Day 53
Onward, Christian Soldiers 109
Our Father 110
Our Giving-to-God Song 174
Our God, Our Help 211

Pass It On 111
Pass Me Not 217
Pentecostal Power 48
Praise God from Whom All Blessings Flow 54
Praise Him 25
Praise Him! Praise Him! 64
Praise, My Soul 44
Praise the Lord (Lenten Acclamation) 139
Praise the Lord 143
Praise to the Holiest 65
Praise to the Lord, the Almighty 66
Praise to You, Lord Jesus Christ 1 141
Praise to You, Lord Jesus Christ 2 142
Praise to You, O Lord 140b
Prayer After We Eat 185
Prayer Before We Eat 184
Prayer of St. Francis 112

Rock of Ages 216

Sanctus (Orbis Factor) 230
Sanctus (de Angelis) 235
See the Paraclete 208
Silent Night 14
Sing of Mary 76
Sing Out to God 114
Softly Now the Light of Day 219
Song for Evening 113
Song in the Fields 223
Songs of Thankfulness and Praise 20
Sons of God 83
Spirit Creator 221

Spirit of the Living God 49
Spirit of Truth and Light 50
Standin' in the Need of Prayer 115
Stand Up for Jesus 224

Take and Eat 86
Take My Life 116
The Children of the Hebrews 31
The Church's One Foundation 69
The First Noel 15
The Holy Trinity 225
The Lord Be Praised! 144
The Lord's Prayer 1 158
The Lord's Prayer 2 159
The Old Rugged Cross 28
The Saints Proclaim God's Power 78
The Savior Is Waiting 118
The Small Child Checks Up at Night 187
The Small Child Makes His Own Prayer 176
The Small Child Pays a Visit 175
The Small Child Prays for His Country 186
The Small Child Prays for Others 178
The Small Child Sings 168
The Star-Spangled Banner 126
The Strife Is O'er 45
There Is a Balm in Gilead 117
Thou Didst Leave Thy Throne 16
To God Be the Glory 67
To Jesus Christ, Our Sov'reign King 58
Trust and Obey 119
Turn Your Eyes Upon Jesus 26

We Commemorate Your Death 153
We Plow the Fields 120
We Pray for Our Priest 177
We Thank Thee, O Our Father 215
Were You There? 35
What a Friend 121
When Evening Shades Are Falling 214
When I Survey the Wondrous Cross 36
When I Was Baptized 170
When Morning Gilds the Skies 218
When We Eat This Bread 151

Yours Are the Heavens 17

Topical Index

TOPICAL INDEX

This index does not exhaust the manner in which this hymn book may be used. The experienced choir director will discover many other uses for the hymns.

No attempt has been made to list entrance or recessional songs. We would like to suggest, however, that some of the brief seasonal hymns (e.g. In the Beginning Was the Word, No. 2; Bringing Myrrh, Gold and Incense, No. 19) lend themselves to recessionals, especially on weekdays.

No special hymns for the preparation rite have been listed. This is the ideal time for silence during the Celebration of the Eucharist. The people may respond to the brief prayers of the celebrant.

The most important songs at the Eucharist are the acclamations, especially the Holy, Holy, Holy Lord following the Preface. Traditionally this has always belonged to the people, and ideally it should be sung.

Song during the Communion Procession is also important. The suggested Communion hymns in this book have refrains that the people can easily sing while the choir sings the verses.

ADVENT

Come, Thou Long Expected Jesus 1
In the Beginning Was the Word 2
In the Fullness of Time 3
Maranatha 4
O Come, O Come, Emmanuel 5
On Jordan's Bank 6

ASPERGES (Rite of Blessing and Sprinkling of Water)

Grafted on the Vine 101

ASSUMPTION OF MARY

Hail, Holy Queen 71
Hymn of the Angels 206
O Virgin Most Wise 77

BAPTISM

Grafted on the Vine 101

BENEDICTION OF THE BLESSED SACRAMENT

Humbly Let Us Voice Our Homage 167
O Saving Victim 166

BLESSED SACRAMENT

Behold the Living Bread 55
Humbly Let Us Voice Our Homage (Benediction) 167
Jesus, My Lord, My God 213

Only a Veil 24
O Saving Victim (Benediction) 166

CHILDREN'S SONGS
A Child's Prayer 183
Dear Saint Joseph 181
God Gives Us an Angel 179
Going Home Song 182
I'm So Glad 169
In Praise of God 171
Jesus, Love Is in Your Heart 172
Jesus, on the Cross You Died 173
Mary, My Mother 180
Our Giving-to-God Song 174
Prayer After We Eat 185
Prayer Before We Eat 184
The Small Child Checks Up at Night 187
The Small Child Makes His Own Prayer 176
The Small Child Pays a Visit 175
The Small Child Prays for His Country 186
The Small Child Prays for Others 178
The Small Child Sings 168
We Pray for Our Priest 177
When I Was Baptized 170

CHRIST THE KING
All Glory, Laud, and Honor 30
All Hail the Power of Jesus' Name 21
Crown Him With Many Crowns 57
Glorious God 59
He Lives 41
Praise, My Soul 44
To Jesus Christ, Our Sov'reign King 58

CHRISTIAN BURIAL
Grafted on the Vine 101
I Am the Bread of Life 85
I Saw the New Jerusalem 104
The Strife Is O'er 45

CHRISTMAS
All the Ends of the Earth 7
Angels from the Realms of Glory 190
Angels We Have Heard on High 8
Away in a Manger 194

Go, Tell It on the Mountain (Spiritual) 9
Good King Wenceslas 193
Hark, the Herald Angels Sing 11
Joy to the World 10
O Come, All Ye Faithful 13
O Little Town of Bethlehem 12
Silent Night 14
The First Noel 15
Thou Didst Leave Thy Throne 16
Yours Are the Heavens 17

CHURCH
Faith of Our Fathers 68
Onward, Christian Soldiers 109
The Church's One Foundation 69

COMMUNION
Canticle of the Gift 80
Christians, Let Us Love One Another 81
Communion Song — In the Upper Room 82
God and Man at Table Are Sat Down 87
How Lovely Is Your Dwelling Place (Ps. 84) 84
I Am the Bread of Life 85
Sons of God 83
Take and Eat 86

CONFIRMATION (See Holy Spirit)

DISMISSAL
Go Now and Live for the Savior 100
Lord, Dismiss Us 92

EASTER
At the Lamb's High Feast 37
Be Joyful, Mary 39
Christ the Lord Is Ris'n Today 38
He Lives 41
Jesus Christ Is Ris'n Today 42
O Queen of Heaven 43
Praise, My Soul 44
The Strife Is O'er 45

EPIPHANY
As With Gladness Men of Old 18
Bringing Myrrh, Gold and Incense 19

Songs of Thankfulness and Praise 20

EVENING
As the Dewy Shades of Even 198
Now the Day Is Over 197
Softly Now the Light of Day 219
Song for Evening 113

FRUITS OF THE EARTH
We Plow the Fields 120

GENERAL
A Mighty Fortress Is Our God 88
Abide With Me 189
All Things Through Christ 89
Amazing Grace! 90
Amen (Spiritual) 91
Art Thou Weary? 195
Blessed Is He 93
Bring Back the Springtime 94
Bringing in the Sheaves 95
Come as a Child 96
Fill My Cup, Lord 97
Follow Me 98
For All the Blessings 99
Go Now and Live for the Savior 100
Grafted on the Vine 101
Hark, Hark, My Soul 226
Heart Speaks to Heart 102
He Leadeth Me 203
Hymn for Renewal 103
Hymn to the Pope 207
I Need Thee Every Hour 204
I Saw the New Jerusalem 104
Jesus Loves Me, This I Know 220
Joyful, Joyful, We Adore Thee 105
Lead, Kindly Light 212
Let All That Is Within Me Cry Holy 106
Let There Be Peace on Earth 107
Like a Lamb Who Needs the Shepherd 108
Lord, Dismiss Us 92
My God, How Wonderful 192
Nearer, My God, to Thee 210
Onward, Christian Soldiers 109
Our Father 110

Our God, Our Help 211
Pass It On 111
Prayer of St. Francis 112
Rock of Ages 216
Song for Evening 113
Sing Out to God 114
Song in the Fields 223
Stand Up for Jesus 224
Standin' in the Need of Prayer (Spiritual) 115
Take My Life 116
There Is a Balm in Gilead (Spiritual) 117
The Savior Is Waiting 118
Trust and Obey 119
We Plow the Fields 120
What a Friend 121

JESUS
All Hail the Power of Jesus' Name 21
Gentle Like You 22
Jesus, Lover of My soul 209
Jesus Loves Me, This I Know 220
Jesus, the Only Thought of Thee 23
Only a Veil 24
Praise Him 25
Turn Your Eyes Upon Jesus 26

LABOR DAY
O Workman Worthy 79

LENT (See also Passion)
Have Mercy on Me 29
Lord Who Throughout These Forty Days 27
The Old Rugged Cross 28

HOLY SPIRIT
Breathe on Me, Breath of God 46
Come, Holy Ghost 47
Pentecostal Power 48
See the Paraclete 208
Spirit Creator 221
Spirit of the Living God 49
Spirit of Truth and Light 50

HOLY TRINITY
All People That on Earth Do Dwell 191

God Father, Praise and Glory 51
Holy, Holy, Holy! Lord God Almighty 52
On This Day 53
Praise God from Whom All Blessings Flow 54
The Holy Trinity 225

IMMACULATE CONCEPTION (See also Patriotic)
Immaculate Mary 72

JOSEPH, ST.
Dear Saint Joseph (for Children) 181
Holy Patron 205
O Workman Worthy 79

MARY
As the Dewy Shades of Even 198
Be Joyful, Mary 39
Hail, Holy Queen 71
Hail Mary 70
Heart of Mary 202
Hymn of the Angels 206
Immaculate Mary 72
Indian Magnificat 73
Mary, My Mother (for Children) 180
Mary's Joy 74
Mother of the Americas 75
O Purest of Creatures 199
O Queen of Heaven 43
O Virgin Most Wise 77
Sing of Mary 76
When Evening Shades Are Falling 214

MASS ("Ordinary Parts")
Alleluias 133-140
Amen 154-157
Credo III (from Kyriale) 229
Doxology after the Lord's Prayer 160,161
Glory to God 130, 131, 132
Gospel Acclamations (Alleluias) 133-140
Gospel Acclamations (for Lent) 139-144
Great Amen 91,154,157
Holy, Holy, Holy Lord 145, 146, 147
Lamb of God 162-165
Lord, Have Mercy 127, 128, 129
Memorial Acclamations 148-153

Missa de Angelis (No. 8 in Kyriale) 233
Orbis Factor (No. 11 in Kyriale) 227
The Lord's Prayer 110, 158, 159

MORNING
Lord God of Morning 196
When Morning Gilds the Skies 218

OUR LADY OF GUADALUPE
Mother of the Americas 75

PALM SUNDAY
All Glory, Laud, and Honor 30
The Children of the Hebrews 31

PASSION OF JESUS
Alas! And Did My Savior Bleed? 188
At the Cross Her Station Keeping 33
Ballad of the Passion 32
Jesus on the Cross You Died (for Children) 173
O Sacred Head 34
Were You There? (Spiritual) 35
When I Survey the Wondrous Cross 36

PATRIOTIC
America 123
America, the Beautiful 122
Battle Hymn of the Republic 124
Beyond a Dream 125
God Bless Our Native Land 222
The Star-Spangled Banner 126

PENANCE SERVICE (See also Praise and Thanksgiving)
Bring Back the Springtime 94
Go Now and Live for the Savior 100
Let There Be Peace on Earth 107
My God How Wonderful 192
Pass Me Not 217
Prayer of St. Francis 112
Rock of Ages 216

PRAISE AND THANKSGIVING
For All the Blessings 99
Glorious God 59
Great Is the Lord (Mission Song) 60

Holy God, We Praise Thy Name 61
Now Thank We All Our God 62
O Lord, We Bless You 63
Praise Him in the Morning 25
Praise Him! Praise Him! 64
Praise to the Holiest 65
Praise to the Lord, the Almighty 66
To God be the Glory 67
We Thank Thee, O Our Father 215
When Morning Gilds the Skies 218

RELIGIOUS RECEPTION AND PROFESSION (See also Holy Spirit)
Follow Me 98
I Saw the New Jerusalem 104
Take My Life 116

ROSARY
Ballad of the Passion (Sorrowful Mysteries) 32
Mary's Joy (Joyful Mysteries) 74

SACRAMENT OF THE SICK
Hark, Hark, My Soul 226
Rock of Ages 216
Softly Now the Light of Day 219
When Evening Shades Are Falling 214

SACRED HEART OF JESUS
Learn of Me 56

SAINTS
The Saints Proclaim God's Power 78

SPIRITUALS
Amen 91
Go Down, Moses 200
Go, Tell It on the Mountain 9
Nobody Knows the Trouble I've Seen 201
Standin' in the Need of Prayer 115
There Is a Balm in Gilead 117
Were You There? 35

THANKSGIVING (See Praise and Thanksgiving)

THANKSGIVING DAY
For All the Blessings 99
We Plow the Fields 120

Order of the Mass

Introductory Rite

Stand

ENTRANCE SONG

GREETINGS

Priest: In the name of the Father, and of the Son, and of the Holy Spirit.
People: Amen

(A) Priest: The grace of our Lord Jesus Christ and the love of God and the fellowship of the Holy Spirit be with you all.
People: And also with you.

(B) Priest: The grace and peace of God our Father and the Lord Jesus Christ be with you.
People: Blessed be God the Father of our Lord Jesus Christ, or **And also with you.**

(C) Priest: The Lord be with you.
People: And also with you.

PENITENTIAL RITE

(A) Priest: My brothers and sisters, to prepare ourselves to celebrate the sacred mysteries, let us call to mind our sins.

(Brief silence)

Priest and People:
I confess to almighty God,
and to you, my brothers and sisters,
that I have sinned through my own fault (All strike breast)
in my thoughts and in my words,
in what I have done,
and in what I have failed to do;
and I ask blessed Mary, ever virgin,
all the angels and saints,
and you my brothers and sisters
to pray for me to the Lord our God.

Priest: May almighty God have mercy on us,
forgive us our sins,
and bring us to everlasting life.
People: Amen.

(B) Priest: My brothers and sisters, to prepare ourselves to celebrate the sacred mysteries, let us call to mind our sins.

(Brief silence)

Lord, we have sinned against you:
Lord, have mercy.
People: Lord, have mercy.
Priest: Lord, show us your mercy and love.
People: And grant us your salvation.
Priest: May almighty God have mercy on us,
forgive us our sins,
and bring us to everlasting life.
People: Amen.

(C) Priest: My brothers and sisters, to prepare ourselves to celebrate the sacred mysteries, let us call to mind our sins.

(Brief silence)

You were sent to heal the contrite:
Lord, have mercy.
People: Lord, have mercy
Priest: You came to call sinners:
Christ, have mercy.
People: Christ, have mercy.
Priest: You plead for us at the right hand of the Father:
Lord, have mercy.
People: Lord, have mercy.

Priest: May almighty God have mercy on us,
forgive us our sins,
and bring us to everlasting life.
People: Amen.

KYRIE

Priest: Lord, have mercy.
People: Lord, have mercy.
Priest: Christ, have mercy.
People: Christ, have mercy.
Priest: Lord, have mercy.
People: Lord, have mercy.

GLORIA

Priest and People say or sing:
Glory to God in the highest,
and peace to his people on earth.
Lord God, heavenly King,
almighty God and Father,
we worship you, we give you thanks,
we praise you for your glory.
Lord Jesus Christ, only Son of the Father,
Lord God, Lamb of God,
you take away the sin of the world:
have mercy on us;
you are seated at the right hand of the Father:
receive our prayer.
For you alone are the Holy One,
you alone are the Lord,
you alone are the Most High,
Jesus Christ,
with the Holy Spirit,
in the glory of God the Father. Amen.

OPENING PRAYER

Priest: Let us pray.
People: Amen.

Liturgy of the Word

it

READING I

eople: **Thanks be to God.**

ESPONSORIAL PSALM

EADING II

tand

ALLELUIA

antor: Alleluia.
eople: **Alleluia.**
antor: (Versicles vary)
eople: **Alleluia.**

GOSPEL

iest: The Lord be with you.
eople: **And also with you.**
iest: + A reading from the holy gospel according to . . .
ople: **Glory to you, Lord.**

ople: **Praise to you, Lord Jesus Christ.**

t

HOMILY

nd

PROFESSION OF FAITH

iest and People:
e believe in one God,
the Father, the Almighty,
maker of heaven and earth,
of all that is seen and unseen.
e believe in one Lord, Jesus Christ,
the only Son of God,
eternally begotten of the Father,
God from God, Light from Light,
true God from true God,
begotten not made, one in Being with the Father.
Through him all things were made.
r us men and for our salvation
he came down from heaven:
(All bow at the following words up to: and became man.)
the power of the Holy Spirit
he was born of the Virgin Mary, and became man.
r our sake he was crucified under Pontius Pilate;
he suffered, died and was buried.
On the third day he rose again
in fulfillment of the Scriptures;
he ascended into heaven
and is seated at the right hand of the Father.
He will come again in glory to judge the living and the dead,
and his kingdom will have no end.

We believe in the Holy Spirit, the Lord, the giver of life,
who proceeds from the Father and the Son.
With the Father and the Son he is worshiped and glorified.
He has spoken through the Prophets.
We believe in one holy catholic and apostolic Church.
We acknowledge one baptism for the forgiveness of sins.
We look for the resurrection of the dead,
and the life of the world to come. Amen.

GENERAL INTERCESSIONS: **Prayer of the Faithful**

Liturgy of the Eucharist

Presentation of the Gifts

Sit — **PREPARATION SONG or PEOPLE'S RESPONSES**

Priest: Blessed are you, Lord, God of all creation. Through your goodness, we have this bread to offer, which earth has given and human hands have made. It will become for us the bread of life.
People: Blessed be God forever.

Priest: Blessed are you Lord, God of all creation. Through your goodness we have this wine to offer, fruit of the vine and work of human hands. It will become our spiritual drink.
People: Blessed be God forever.

Stand — **PRAYER OVER THE GIFTS**

People: Amen.

Priest: Pray, brethren, that our sacrifice
may be acceptable to
God, the almighty Father.
People: May the Lord accept the sacrifice at your hands
for the praise and glory of his name,
for our good, and the good of all his Church.

EUCHARISTIC PRAYER

Priest: The Lord be with you.
People: And also with you.
Priest: Lift up your hearts.
People: We lift them up to the Lord.
Priest: Let us give thanks to the Lord our God.
People: It is right to give him thanks and praise.

PREFACE

SANCTUS

Priest and People:
Holy, holy, holy Lord, God of power and might,
heaven and earth are full of your glory.
Hosanna in the highest.
Blessed is he who comes in the name of the Lord.
Hosanna in the highest.

EUCHARISTIC PRAYER I

THE ROMAN CANON

Ve come to you, Father
vith praise and thanksgiving,
hrough Jesus Christ your Son.
'hrough him we ask you to accept and bless +
hese gifts we offer you in sacrifice.
Ve offer them for your holy catholic Church,
vatch over it, Lord, and guide it;
rant it peace and unity throughout the world.
Ve offer them for N. our Pope,
or N. our bishop,
nd for all who hold and teach the catholic faith
hat comes to us from the apostles.
Remember, Lord, your people,
specially those for whom we now pray, N. and N.
Remember all of us gathered here before you.
'ou know how firmly we believe in you
nd dedicate ourselves to you.
Ve offer you this sacrifice of praise
or ourselves and those who are dear to us.
Ve pray to you, our living and true God,
or our well-being and redemption.
n union with the whole Church
e honor Mary,
he ever-virgin mother of Jesus Christ our Lord and God.
Ve honor Joseph, her husband,
he apostles and martyrs Peter and Paul, Andrew,
James, John, Thomas,
ames, Philip,
artholomew, Matthew, Simon and Jude;
e honor Linus, Cletus, Clement, Sixtus,
ornelius, Cyprian, Lawrence, Chrysogonus,
ohn and Paul, Cosmas and Damian)
nd all the saints.
Iay their merits and prayers
ain us your constant help and protection.
Through Christ our Lord, Amen.)
'ather, accept this offering
om your whole family.
irant us your peace in this life,
ave us from final damnation,
and count us among those you have chosen.
(Through Christ our Lord, Amen.)
Bless and approve our offering:
make it acceptable to you,
an offering in spirit and in truth.
Let it become for us
the body + and blood of Jesus Christ,
your only Son, our Lord.
The day before he suffered
he took bread in his sacred hands
and looking up to heaven,
to you, his almighty Father,
he gave you thanks and praise.
He broke the bread,
gave it to his disciples, and said:
Take this, all of you, and eat it:
this is my body which will be given up for you.
When supper was ended,
he took the cup.
Again he gave you thanks and praise,
gave the cup to his disciples, and said:
Take this, all of you, and drink from it:
this is the cup of my blood,
the blood of the new and everlasting covenant.
It will be shed for you and for all men
so that sins may be forgiven.
Do this in memory of me.
Let us proclaim the mystery of faith

Christ has died,
Christ is risen,
Christ will come again.

Dying you destroyed our death,
rising you restored our life.
Lord Jesus, come in glory.

When we eat this bread and drink this cup, we proclaim your death, Lord Jesus, until you come in glory.

Lord, by your cross and resurrection
you have set us free.
You are the Savior of the world.

Father, we celebrate the memory of Christ, your Son.
We, your people and your ministers,
recall his passion,
his resurrection from the dead,
and his ascension into glory;
and from the many gifts you have given us
we offer to you, God of glory and majesty,

this holy and perfect sacrifice;
the bread of life
and the cup of eternal salvation.
Look with favor on these offerings
and accept them as once you accepted
the gifts of your servant Abel,
the sacrifice of Abraham, our father in faith,
and the bread and wine offered by your priest Melchisedech.
Almighty God,
we pray that your angel may take this sacrifice
to your altar in heaven.
Then, as we receive from this altar
the sacred body and blood of your Son,
let us be filled with every grace and blessing.
(Through Christ our Lord. Amen.)
Remember, Lord, those who have died
and have gone before us marked with the sign of faith,
especially those for whom we now pray, N. and N.
May these, and all who sleep in Christ,
find in your presence
light, happiness, and peace.
(Through Christ our Lord, Amen.)
For ourselves, too, we ask
some share in the fellowship of your apostles and martyrs,
with John the Baptist, Stephen, Matthias, Barnabas,
(Ignatius, Alexander, Marcellinus, Peter,
Felicity, Perpetua, Agatha, Lucy,
Agnes, Cecilia, Anastasia)
and all the saints.
Though we are sinners,
we trust in your mercy and love.
Do not consider what we truly deserve
but grant us your forgiveness.
Through Christ our Lord
you gave us all these gifts.
You fill them with life and goodness
you bless them and make them holy.

(Turn forward to the Doxology on page 32)

EUCHARISTIC PRAYER II

Father, it is our duty and our salvation,
always and everywhere
to give you thanks
through your beloved son, Jesus Christ.
He is the Word through whom you made the universe,
the Savior you sent to redeem us.
By the power of the Holy Spirit
he took flesh and was born of the Virgin Mary.
For our sake he opened his arms on the cross;
he put an end to death
and revealed the resurrection.
In this he fulfilled your will
and won for you a holy people.
And so we join the angels and the saints
in proclaiming your glory
as we sing (say):

**Holy, holy, holy Lord, God of power and might, heaven and earth are full of your glory.
Hosanna in the highest. Blessed is he who comes in the name of the Lord.
Hosanna in the highest.**

Lord, you are holy indeed,
the fountain of all holiness.
Let your Spirit come upon these gifts to make them holy,
so that they may become for us
the body + and blood of our Lord Jesus Christ.
Before he was given up to death,
a death he freely accepted,
he took bread and gave you thanks.
He broke the bread,
gave it to his disciples, and said:

*Take this, all of you, and eat it:
this is my body which will be given up for you.*

When supper was ended, he took the cup.
Again he gave you thanks and praise,
gave the cup to his disciples, and said:

*Take this, all of you, and drink from it:
this is the cup of my blood,
the blood of the new and everlasting covenant.
It will be shed for you and for all men
so that sins may be forgiven.
Do this in memory of me.*

Let us proclaim the mystery of faith:

hrist has died,
hrist is risen,
hrist will come again.

ying you destroyed our death,
ing you restored our life.
ord Jesus, come in glory.

hen we eat this bread and drink this p, we proclaim your death, Lord sus, until you come in glory.

ord, by your cross and resurrection
u have set us free.
ou are the Savior of the world.

memory of his death and resurrection,
e offer you, Father, this life-giving bread,
is saving cup.
'e thank you for counting us worthy
stand in your presence and serve you.
lay all of us who share in the body and blood of Christ
e brought together in unity by the Holy Spirit.
ord, remember your Church throughout the world;
make us grow in love,
together with N. our Pope,
N. our bishop, and all the clergy.*
Remember our brothers and sisters
who have gone to their rest
in the hope of rising again;
bring them and all the departed
into the light of your presence.
Have mercy on us all;
make us worthy to share eternal life
with Mary, the virgin Mother of God,
with the apostles,
and with all the saints who have done your will throughout the ages.
May we praise you in union with them,
and give you glory
through your Son, Jesus Christ.

(Turn forward to the
Doxology on page 32)

**In Masses for the Dead the following may be added:*
Remember N., whom you have called from this life.
In baptism he (she) died with Christ:
may he (she) also share his resurrection.

EUCHARISTIC PRAYER III

ather, you are holy indeed,
nd all creation rightly gives you praise.
ll life, all holiness comes from you
rough your Son, Jesus Christ our Lord,
y the working of the Holy Spirit.
rom age to age you gather a people to yourself,
that from east to west
perfect offering may be made
the glory of your name.
nd so, Father, we bring you these gifts.
'e ask you to make them holy by the power of your Spirit,
at they may become the body + and blood
your Son, our Lord Jesus Christ,
whose command we celebrate this eucharist.
n the night he was betrayed,
took bread and gave you thanks and praise.
e broke the bread, gave it to his disciples, and said:
ake this, all of you, and eat it:
is is my body which will be given up for you.
When supper was ended, he took the cup.
Again he gave you thanks and praise,
gave the cup to his disciples, and said:
Take this, all of you, and drink from it:
this is the cup of my blood,
the blood of the new and everlasting covenant.
It will be shed for you and for all men
so that sins may be forgiven.
Do this in memory of me.
Let us proclaim the mystery of faith:

Christ has died.
Christ is risen.
Christ will come again.

Dying you destroyed our death,
rising you restored our life.
Lord Jesus, come in glory.

When we eat this bread and drink this cup, we proclaim your death, Lord Jesus. until you come in glory.

Lord, by your cross and resurrection
you have set us free.
You are the Savior of the world.

Father, calling to mind the death your Son endured for our salvation,

his glorious resurrection and ascension into heaven,
and ready to greet him when he comes again,
we offer you in thanksgiving this holy and living sacrifice.
Look with favor on your Church's offering,
and see the Victim whose death has reconciled us to yourself.
Grant that we, who are nourished by his body and blood,
may be filled with his Holy Spirit,
and become one body, one spirit in Christ.
May he make us an everlasting gift to you
and enable us to share in the inheritance of your saints,
with Mary, the virgin Mother of God;
with the apostles, the martyrs,
(Saint N.) and all your saints,
on whose constant intercession we rely for help.
Lord, may this sacrifice, which has made our peace with you,
advance the peace and salvation of all the world.
Strengthen in faith and love your pilgrim Church on earth:
your servant, Pope N., our bishop N.,
and all the bishops,
with the clergy and the entire people your Son has gained for you.
Father, hear the prayers of the family you have gathered here before you.
In mercy and love unite all your ch dren
wherever they may be.*
Welcome into your kingdom our d parted brothers and sisters,
and all who have left this world in yo friendship.
We hope to enjoy forever the vision your glory,
through Christ our Lord, from who all good things come.

(Turn forward to the Doxology on page 32)

*In Masses for the Dead the followi may be added:
Remember N.
In baptism he (she) died with Christ:
may he (she) also share his resurr tion,
when Christ will raise our mor bodies
and make them like his own in glory.
Welcome into your kingdom our parted brothers and sisters
and all who have left this world in yc friendship.
There we hope to share in your glory
when every tear will be wiped away.
On that day we shall see you, our G as you are.
We shall become like you
and praise you forever through Ch our Lord,
from whom all good things come.

EUCHARISTIC PRAYER IV

Father in heaven, it is right that we should give you thanks and glory:
you alone are God, living and true.
Through all eternity you live in unapproachable light.
Source of life and goodness, you have created all things, to fill your creatures with every blessing
and lead all men to the joyful vision of your light.
Countless hosts of angels stand before you to do your will;
they look upon your splendor
and praise you, night and day.
United with them, and in the name of every creature under heaven,
we too praise your glory as we sing (say):

Holy, holy, holy Lord, God of power and might, heaven and earth are full of your glory. Hosanna in the highest. Blessed is who comes in the name of the Lord. Hosanna in the highest.

Father, we acknowledge yc greatness:
all your actions show your wisdom a love.
You formed man in your own likene
and set him over the whole world
to serve you, his creator,
and to rule over all creatures.
Even when he disobeyed you and l your friendship
you did not abandon him to the pov of death,
but helped all men to seek and fi you.
Again and again you offered a co nant to man,
and through the prophets taught h to hope for salvation.

ther, you so loved the world
it in the fullness of time you sent
your only Son to be our Savior.
was conceived through the power
of the Holy Spirit, and born of the
Virgin Mary,
nan like us in all things but sin.
the poor he proclaimed the good
news of salvation,
prisoners, freedom,
d to those in sorrow, joy.
fulfillment of your will
gave himself up to death;
t by rising from the dead,
destroyed death and restored life.
d that we might live no longer for
ourselves but for him,
sent the Holy Spirit from you, Father,
his first gift to those who believe,
complete his work on earth
d bring us the fullness of grace.
ther, may this Holy Spirit sanctify
these offerings.
t them become the body + and
blood of Jesus Christ our Lord
we celebrate the great mystery
ich he left us as an everlasting covenant.
always loved those who were his
own in the world.
ien the time came for him to be
glorified by you, his heavenly Father,
showed the depth of his love.
iile they were at supper,
took bread, said the blessing, broke
the bread,
d gave it to his disciples, saying:

ke this, all of you, and eat it:
s is my body which will be given up for
you.

the same way, he took the cup, filled
with wine.
gave you thanks, and giving the cup
o his disciples, said:

ke this, all of you, and drink from it:
s is the cup of my blood,
blood of the new and everlasting cov-
enant.
will be shed for you and for all men
that sins may be forgiven.
this in memory of me.

: us proclaim the mystery of faith:

Christ has died,
Christ is risen,
Christ will come again.

Dying you destroyed our death,
rising you restored our life.
Lord Jesus, come in glory.

When we eat this bread and drink this cup, we proclaim your death, Lord Jesus, until you come in glory.

Lord, by your cross and resurrection
you have set us free.
You are the Savior of the world.

Father, we now celebrate this memorial of our redemption.
We recall Christ's death, his descent among the dead,
his resurrection, and his ascension to your right hand;
and, looking forward to his coming in glory, we offer you his body and blood,
the acceptable sacrifice which brings salvation to the whole world.
Lord, look upon this sacrifice which you have given to your Church;
and by your Holy Spirit, gather all who share this bread and wine
into the one body of Christ, a living sacrifice of praise.
Lord, remember those for whom we offer this sacrifice,
especially N. our Pope,
N. our bishop, and bishops and clergy everywhere.
Remember those who take part in this offering,
those here present and all your people,
and all who seek you with a sincere heart.
Remember those who have died in the peace of Christ
and all the dead whose faith is known to you alone.
Father, in your mercy grant also to us, your children,
to enter into our heavenly inheritance
in the company of the Virgin Mary, the Mother of God,
and your apostles and saints.
Then, in your kingdom, freed from the corruption of sin and death,
we shall sing your glory with every creature through Christ our Lord,
through whom you give us everything that is good.

DOXOLOGY OF EUCHARISTIC PRAYER

Priest: Through him,
with him,
in him,
in the unity of the
Holy Spirit,
all glory and honor
is yours,
almighty Father,
forever and ever.
People: Amen.

Communion Rite

Stand

LORD'S PRAYER

Priest: Let us pray with confidence to the Father in the words our Savior gave us:

Priest and People:
Our Father, who art in heaven,
hallowed be thy Name,
thy kingdom come,
thy will be done,
on earth as it is in heaven.
Give us this day our daily bread,
and forgive us our trespasses
as we forgive those who trespass against us,
and lead us not into temptation,
but deliver us from evil.

Priest: Deliver us, Lord, from every evil, and grant us peace in our day. In your mercy keep us free from sin and protect us from all anxiety as we wait in joyful hope for the coming of our Savior, Jesus Christ.
People: For the kingdom, the power, and the glory are yours, now and forever.

SIGN OF PEACE

Priest: Lord Jesus Christ, you said to your apostles: I leave you peace, my peace I give you. Look not on our sins, but on the faith of your Church, and grant us the peace and unity of your kingdom where you live forever and ever.
People: Amen.

Priest: The peace of the Lord be with you always.
People: And also with you.

Priest: Let us offer each other the sign of peace. (All make sign according to local custom.)

BREAKING OF THE BREAD

Priest: May this mingling of the body and blood of our Lord Jesus Christ bring eternal life to us who receive it.

People: Lamb of God, you take away the sins of the world:
have mercy on us.
Lamb of God, you take away the sins of the world:
have mercy on us,
Lamb of God, you take away the sins of the world:
grant us peace.

COMMUNION

Priest: This is the Lamb of God who takes away the sins of the world. Happy are those who are called to his supper.

Priest and People:
Lord I am not worthy to receive you,
but only say the word and I shall be healed.

Priest: The body of Christ.
Communicant: Amen.

COMMUNION ANTIPHON

Sit **Silence after Communion or A Song of Praise**

Stand **PRAYER AFTER COMMUNION**

Priest: Let us pray.

People: Amen.

Concluding Rite

ANNOUNCEMENTS

Stand **BLESSING**

(A more solemn blessing or prayer over the people may be said. The people answer **Amen** to each of the invocations or at the end of the prayer. The blessing ends: ". . . remain with you forever." The people respond with **Amen**.)

Priest: The Lord be with you.
People: And also with you.
Priest: May almighty God bless you, the Father, and the Son, + and the Holy Spirit.
People: Amen.

DISMISSAL

Priest: Go in the peace of Christ. (Alleluia)
or
The Mass is ended, go in peace. (Alleluia)
or
Go in peace to love and serve the Lord. (Alleluia)
People: Thanks be to God. (Alleluia)

1 *Come, Thou Long Expected Jesus*

Charles Wesley

Rowland H. Prichard

1. Come, Thou long - ex - pect - ed Je - sus, Born to set Thy
2. Born Thy peo - ple to de - liv - er, Born a child and
peo - ple free; From our fears and sins re - lease us; Let us
yet a King. Born to reign in us for ev - er, Now Thy
find our rest in Thee. Is - rael's Strength and Con - so - la - tion,
gra - cious King - dom bring. By Thine own e - ter - nal Spir - it
Hope of all the earth Thou art; Dear De - sire of
Rule in all our hearts a - lone; By Thine all suf -
ev - ery na - tion, Joy of ev - ery long - ing heart.
fi - cient mer - it, Raise us to Thy glo - rious throne.

2 *In the Beginning Was the Word*

John 1:1, 6-7, 29 C. Uehlein

In the be - gin - ning was the Word, and the
Word was with God, and the Word was God.
And John was sent by God to bear wit - ness to the
Word: "Be - hold the Lamb of God!

3 *In the Fullness of Time*

Galatians 4:4

C. Uehlein

In the full - ness of time God
sent his on - ly Son, born of the
ho - ly vir - gin Ma - ry!

4

Maranatha

Anselm Hollingsworth, OSB

Note: Double bass moves with Guitars — always playing root.

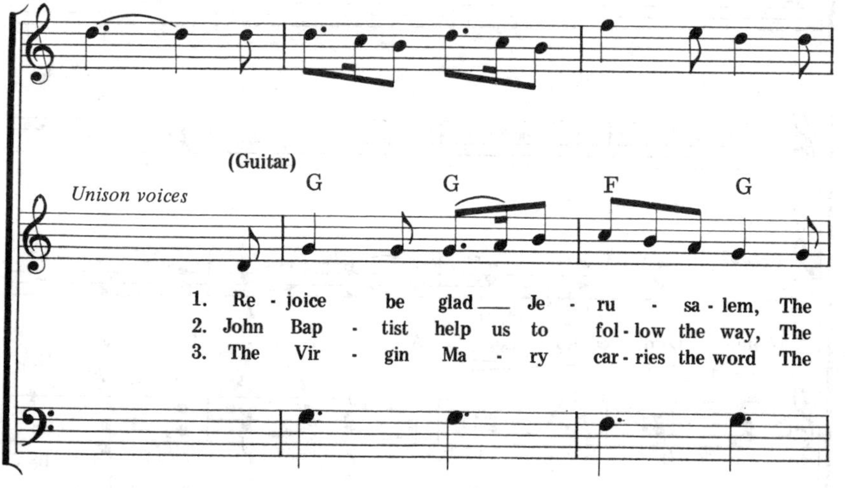
(Guitar)
Unison voices
G G F G
1. Re - joice be glad ___ Je - ru - sa - lem, The
2. John Bap - tist help us to fol - low the way, The
3. The Vir - gin Ma - ry car - ries the word The

F
G
G
G
Lord is near, the Lord is near, Your Sav - ior quick - ly
Lord is near, the Lord is near. Make straight his path for that
Lord is near, the Lord is near. Be still, be calm so his
F
G
F
G
comes — to you, The Lord is near.
glo - ri - ous day, The Lord is near.
voice can be heard, The Lord is near.
Recorder
Refrain (No Guitar, no Recorder)
Voices 1 & 2
Come, Lord, come, Lord, Al - le - lu - ia.
Unison voices
Voices 3 & 4
Come, Lord, come, Lord, Al - le - lu - ia.
1. Be -
2.
3. Lift

(Recorder)
G G F G F
1. hold the most — high king — shall come, The Lord is
2. Turn to the Lord — with joy in your heart, The Lord is
3. *
* Last verse like this:
Voices 1 & 2
G G G F G F
near.
near. Up your voice — Je - ru - sa - lem, The Lord is
(Recorder)
G The Lord is here, the Lord is here!
here!

5 *O Come, O Come, Emmanuel*

Plainsong

1. O come, O come, Em - man - u - el, And ran - som cap - tive
2. O come, thou Wis - dom from on high, Who ord - 'rest all things
3. O come, O come, thou Lord of might, Who to thy tribes on
Is - ra - el, That mourns in lone - ly ex - ile here
might - i - ly; To us the path of knowl - edge show,
Si - nai's height In an - cient times didst give the law,
Un - til the Son of God ap - pear.
And teach us in her ways to go.
In cloud, and ma - jes - ty, and awe.
Refrain
Re - joice! Re - joice!
Em - man - u - el Shall come to thee, O Is - ra - el!

4. O come, thou Rod of Jesse's stem,
From every foe deliver them
That trust thy mighty power to save,
And give them vict'ry o'er the grave.

5. O come, thou Key of David, come,
And open wide our heav'nly home;
Make safe the way that leads on high
And close the path to misery.

6. O come, thou Day-spring from on high,
And cheer us by thy drawing nigh;
Disperse the gloomy clouds of night,
And death's dark shadow put to flight.

7. O come, Desire of nations, bind
In one the hearts of all mankind;
Bid thou our sad divisions cease,
And be thyself our King of Peace.

6 *On Jordan's Bank*

Charles Coffin, 1736

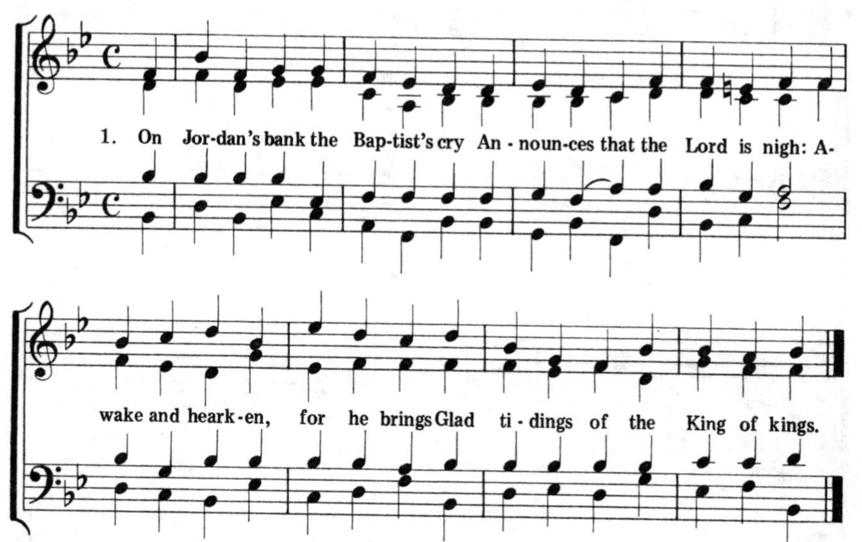
1. On Jor-dan's bank the Bap-tist's cry An - noun-ces that the Lord is nigh: A-
wake and heark-en, for he brings Glad ti - dings of the King of kings.

2. Then cleansed be every breast from sin;
   Make straight the way of God within,
   And let each heart prepare a home
   Where such a mighty guest may come.

3. All praise, eternal Son, to thee,
   Whose advent doth thy people free;
   Whom with the Father we adore
   And Holy Ghost for evermore. Amen.

7 *All the Ends of the Earth*

Ps. 98:3

C. Uehlein

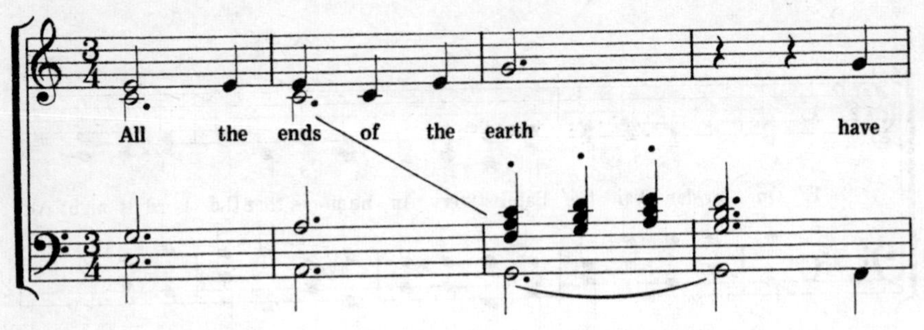
All the ends of the earth have

seen the sal - va - tion by our God!

8 *Angels We Have Heard on High*

Traditional

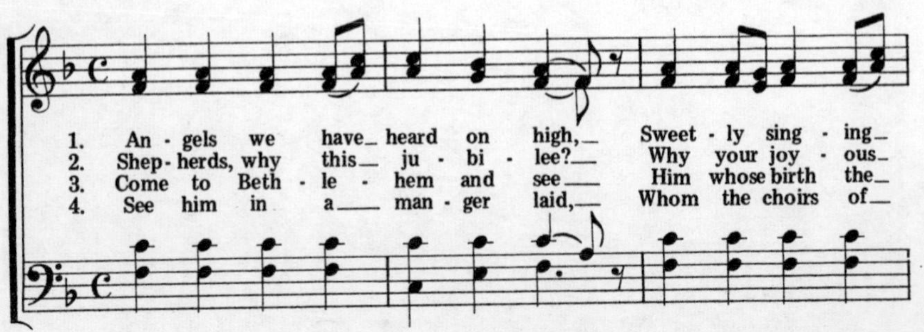
1. An - gels we have heard on high, Sweet - ly sing - ing
2. Shep - herds, why this ju - bi - lee? Why your joy - ous
3. Come to Beth - le - hem and see Him whose birth the
4. See him in a man - ger laid, Whom the choirs of

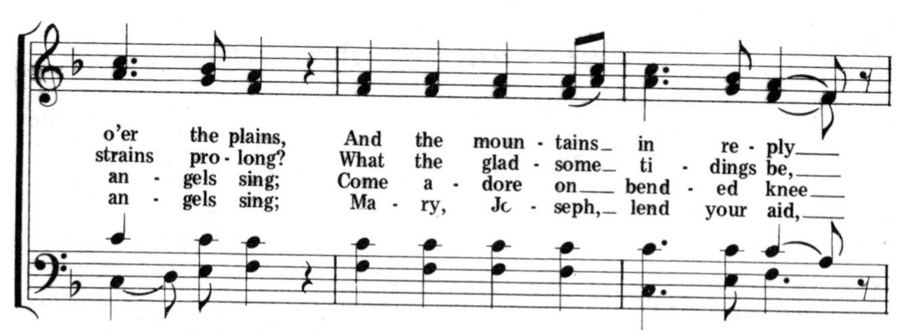
o'er the plains, And the moun - tains_ in re - ply___
strains pro - long? What the glad - some_ ti - dings be,___
an - gels sing; Come a - dore on___ bend - ed knee___
an - gels sing; Ma - ry, Jo - seph,_ lend your aid,___

Ech - o___ back their_ joy - ous strains.
Which in - spire your heav'n - ly song.
Christ the_ Lord, the___ new - born King.
While our_ hearts in___ love we raise.
Glo - - - -
pp

ri - a in ex - cel - sis De - o Glo - -
pp

ri - a in ex - cel - sis De - o.

9 *Go, Tell It on the Mountain*

Spiritual

Refrain
Go, tell it on the moun - tain, O - ver the hills and ev - ery - where;
Go, tell it on the moun - tain That Je - sus Christ is born!
Fine
1. When I was but a sin - ner, I prayed both night and day; I
2. When I be - came a seek - er, I sought both night and day: I
3. The Lord made me a watch - man, up - on a cit - y wall; And
asked the Lord to help me, and He showed me the way.
asked my Lord to help me, and He taught me to pray.
if I am a Chris - tian, I am the least of all.
D.C.

10 *Joy to the World!*

Isaac Watts

George F. Handel

1. Joy to the world! the Lord is come; Let earth re - ceive her King; Let ev - 'ry heart pre - pare Him room, And heav'n and na - ture sing, And heav'n and na - ture sing, And heav'n, and heav'n and na - ture sing.
2. Joy to the earth! the Sav - ior reigns; Let men their songs em - ploy; While fields and floods, rocks, hills and plains Re - peat the sound - ing joy, Re - peat the sound - ing joy, Re - peat, re - peat the sound - ing joy.
3. No more let sins and sor - rows grow, Nor thorns in - fest the ground; He comes to make His bless - ings flow Far as the curse is found, Far as the curse is found, Far as, far as the curse is found.
4. He rules the world with truth and grace, And makes the na - tions prove The glo - ries of His right - eous - ness, And won - ders of His love, And won - ders of His love, And won - ders, and won - ders of His love.
1. And heav'n and na - ture sing And heav'n and na - ture sing.

11 *Hark, the Herald Angels Sing*

Charles Wesley

Felix Mendelssohn

1. Hark! the her - ald an - gels sing,– "Glo - ry to the new- born King:
2. Christ, by high - est heaven a - dored; Christ, the Ev - er - last - ing Lord!
3. Hail the heaven - born Prince of Peace! Hail the Sun of Right - eous - ness!
Peace on earth, and mer - cy mild, God and sin - ners rec - con - ciled!"
Late in time be - hold Him come, Off - spring of the Vir - gin's womb:
Light and life to all He brings, Risen with heal - ing in His wings.
Joy - ful, all ye na - tions, rise_ Join the tri - umph of the skies;
Veiled in flesh the God - head see;_ Hail th'In - car - nate De - i - ty,–
Mild He lays His glo - ry by,— Born that man no more may die,–
With th'an - gel - ic host pro - claim, "Christ is born in Beth - le - hem!"
Pleased as man with men to dwell, Je - sus, our Em - man - u - el.
Born to raise the sons of earth, Born to give them sec - ond birth

Hark! the her-ald an-gels sing, "Glo - ry to the new-born King."

12 *O Little Town of Bethlehem*

Phillips Brooks

Lewis H. Redner

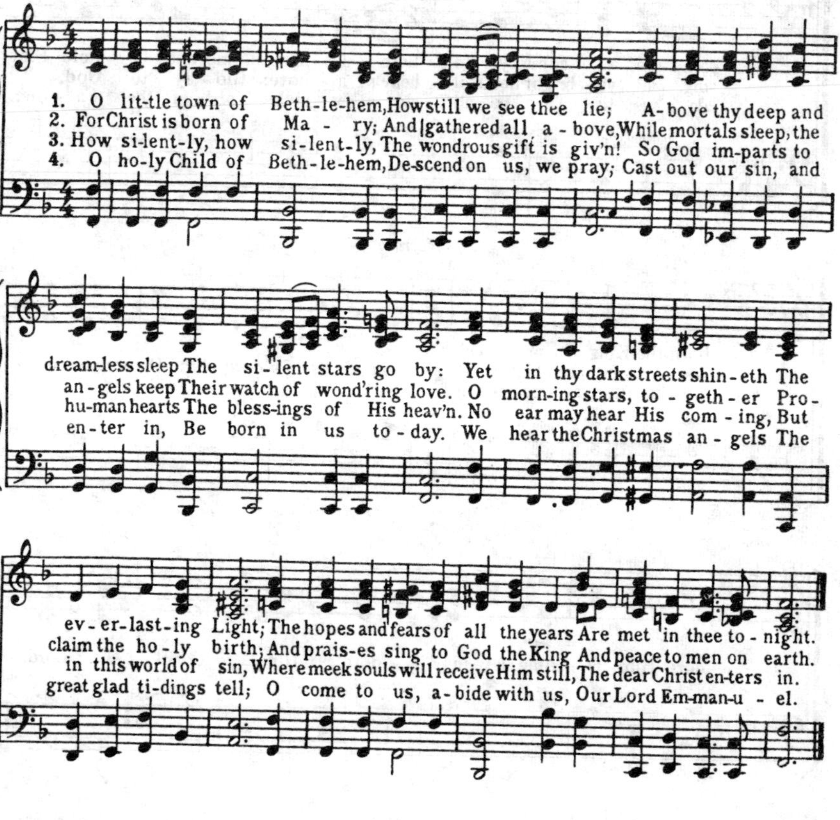

1. O lit-tle town of Beth-le-hem, How still we see thee lie; A-bove thy deep and
2. For Christ is born of Ma - ry; And gathered all a - bove, While mortals sleep, the
3. How si-lent-ly, how si-lent-ly, The wondrous gift is giv'n! So God im-parts to
4. O ho-ly Child of Beth-le-hem, De-scend on us, we pray; Cast out our sin, and

dream-less sleep The si-lent stars go by: Yet in thy dark streets shin-eth The
an-gels keep Their watch of wond'ring love. O morn-ing stars, to-geth-er Pro-
hu-man hearts The bless-ings of His heav'n. No ear may hear His com-ing, But
en-ter in, Be born in us to-day. We hear the Christmas an-gels The

ev-er-last-ing Light; The hopes and fears of all the years Are met in thee to-night.
claim the ho-ly birth; And prais-es sing to God the King And peace to men on earth.
in this world of sin, Where meek souls will receive Him still, The dear Christ en-ters in.
great glad ti-dings tell; O come to us, a-bide with us, Our Lord Em-man-u - el.

13 *O Come, All Ye Faithful*

Tr. by Frederick Oakeley

Wade's Cantus Diversi

1. O come, all ye faith - ful, joy - ful and tri - um - phant, O
2. Sing, choirs of an - gels, sing in ex - ul - ta - tion, O
3. Yea, Lord, we greet Thee, born this hap - py morn - ing,
come ye, O come_ ye to Beth - le - hem; Come and be - hold Him,
sing, all ye bright hosts of heav'n_ a - bove; Glo - ry to God, all
Je - sus, to Thee_ be all glo - ry giv'n; Word of the Fa - ther,
Refrain
born the King of an - gels.
glo - ry in the high - est. O come, let us a - dore Him, O come, let us a -
now in flesh ap - pear - ing.
dore Him, O come, let us a - dore Him,_ Christ,_ the Lord.

14 *Silent Night*

Joseph Möhr

Franz Gruber

1. Si - lent night, ho - ly night, All is calm,
2. Si - lent night, ho - ly night, Shep - herds quake
3. Si - lent night, ho - ly night, Son of God,
1. all is bright 'Round yon Vir - gin Moth - er and Child,
2. at the sight; Glo - ries stream from heav - en a far,
3. love's pure light, Ra - diant, beams from thy ho - ly face,
1. Ho - ly In - fant, so ten - der and mild, Sleep in heav - en - ly
2. Heav'n - ly hosts sing al - le - lu - ia; Christ, the Sav - ior, is
3. With the dawn of re - deem - ing grace, Je - sus, Lord, at thy
1. peace, Sleep in heav - en - ly peace.
2. born, Christ, the Sav - ior, is born!
3. birth, Je - sus, Lord, at thy birth!

15 *The First Noel*

Traditional

1. The first No - el the an - gel did say Was to
2. And by the light of that same Star, Three
3. This Star drew nigh to the north - west, O'er
4. Then en - ter-ed in those wise - men three, Full
cer - tain poor shep - herds in fields as they lay;
wise men came from coun - try far;
Beth - le - hem it took its rest,
rev - 'rent - ly up - on their knee,
In fields where they lay keep - ing their sheep, On a
To seek for a King was their in - tent, And to
And there it did both stop and stay, Right
And of - fered there in His pres - ence, Their

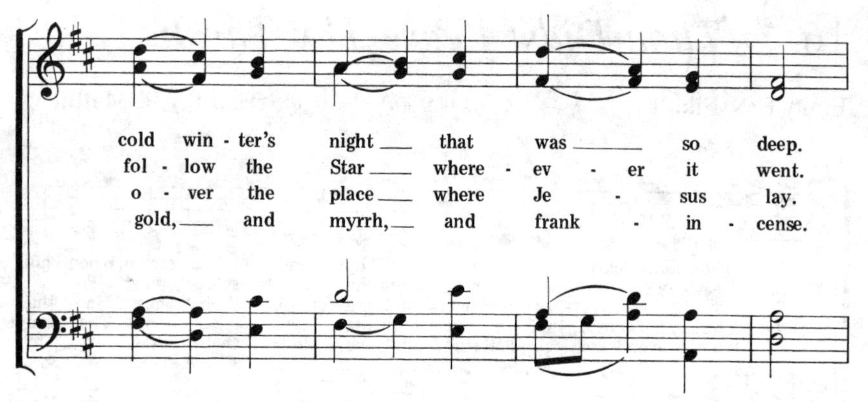
cold win - ter's night that was so deep.
fol - low the Star where - ev - er it went.
o - ver the place where Je - sus lay.
gold, and myrrh, and frank - in - cense.

Refrain
No - el, No - el, No - el, No - el,

Born is the King of Is - ra - el.

16 *Thou Didst Leave Thy Throne*

Emily E. S. Elliott

Timothy R. Matthews

1. Thou didst leave Thy— throne and Thy king - ly— crown, When Thou
2. Heav - en's arch - es— rang when the an - gels— sang, Pro -
3. The— fox - es found rest, and the birds their— nest In the
4. Thou— cam'st, O— Lord, with the liv - ing— word That should
5. When heaven's arch - es shall ring and her choir shall— sing At Thy
cam - est to earth for— me; But in Beth - le - hem's home there was
claim - ing Thy roy - al de - gree; But in low - ly— birth didst Thou
shade of the for - est— tree; But Thy couch was the sod, O Thou
set Thy— peo - ple— free; But with mock - ing— scorn, and with
com - ing to vic - to - ry, Let Thy voice call me home, say - ing,
found no— room For Thy ho - ly Na - tiv - i - ty. O—
come to— earth, And in great hu - mil - i - ty. O—
Son of— God, In the des - erts of Gal - i - lee. O—
crown of— thorn, They— bore Thee to Cal - va - ry. O—
"Yet there is room, There is room at my side for thee!" And my
come to my heart, Lord Je - sus, There is room in my heart for Thee.
come to my heart, Lord Je - sus, There is room in my heart for Thee.
come to my heart, Lord Je - sus, There is room in my heart for Thee.
come to my heart, Lord Je - sus, There is room in my heart for Thee.
heart shall re - joice, Lord Je - sus, When Thou com - est and callest for me.

17 *Yours Are the Heavens*

Ps. 89:12,15

C. Uehlein

Yours are the heav - ens and yours is the
earth; the world and its ful - ness you have
found - ed. Jus - tice and judg - ment are the foun -
da - tion of your throne!
rit.

18 *As with Gladness Men of Old*

Dix — Conrad Kocher, 1838, alt.

1. As with___ glad - ness men of old Did the
2. As with___ joy - ful steps they sped To that
3. As they___ of - fer'd gifts most rare At that
guid - ing star be - hold; As with___ joy they hailed its
low - ly man - ger - bed; There to___ bend the knee be -
man - ger rude and bare; So may___ we with ho - ly
light, Lead - ing on - ward, beam - ing bright; So, most
fore Him whom heav'n and earth a - dore; So may
joy, Pure and free from sin's al - loy; All our
gra - cious Lord, may we Ev - er - more be led to thee.
we with will - ing feet Ev - er seek the mer - cy - seat.
cost - liest trea - sures bring, Christ! to thee, our heav'n - ly King.

19 *Bringing Myrrh, Gold and Incense*

C. Uehlein

Bring - ing myrrh for a tomb, gold for a king,

in - cense for a God, the ma - gi are led by the

light of the star to Christ the Light of the world!

20 *Songs of Thankfulness and Praise*

Christopher Wordsworth, 1862

Jakob Hintze, 1678, alt.

Songs of thank - ful - ness and praise, Je - sus, Lord, to thee we raise,
Man - i - fest at Jor-dan's stream, Pro - phet, Priest, and King su - preme;
Man - i - fest - ed by the star To the sa - ges from a - far;
And at Ca - na, wed - ding guest, In thy God-head man - i - fest;
Branch of roy - al Da - vid's stem In thy birth at Beth - le - hem;
Man - i - fest in power di - vine, Chang-ing wa - ter in - to wine;
An-thems be to thee ad-dressed, God in man made man - i - fest.
An-thems be to thee ad-dressed, God in man made man - i - fest.

21 *All Hail the Power of Jesus' Name*

Edward Perronet, Alt. by John Rippon | Oliver Holden

1. All hail the power of Je - sus' name! Let an - gels pros-trate fall;
2. Ye cho - sen seed of Is rael's race, Ye ran-somed from the fall;
3. Let ev - ery kin - dred, ev - ery tribe, On this ter - res - trial ball,
4. O that with yon - der sa - cred throng We at His feet may fall;

Bring forth the roy - al di - a - dem,
Hail Him who saves you by ___ His ___ grace,
To Him all maj - es - ty ___ as - cribe,
We'll join the ev - er last - ing ___ song,

And crown Him Lord of ___ all; Bring forth the roy - al
And crown Him Lord of ___ all; Hail Him who saves you
And crown Him Lord of ___ all; To Him all maj - es -
And crown Him Lord of ___ all; We'll join the ev - er -

di - a - dem, And crown Him Lord ___ of all.
by ___ His ___ grace, And crown Him Lord ___ of all.
ty ___ as - cribe, And crown Him Lord ___ of all.
last - ing ___ song, And crown Him Lord ___ of all.

Gentle Like You

Charles F. Brown

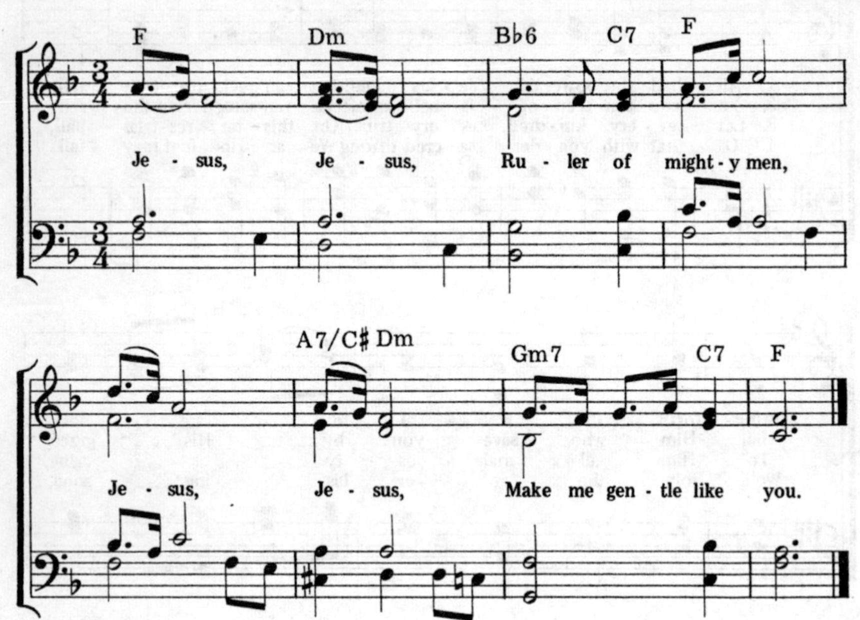
F
Dm
B♭6
C7
F
Je - sus, Je - sus, Ru - ler of might - y men,
A7/C♯ Dm
Gm7
C7
F
Je - sus, Je - sus, Make me gen - tle like you.

2. Jesus, Jesus, Friend to the lonely soul,
   Jesus, Jesus, Love my brother through me.

3. Jesus, Jesus, Shepherd of wandering ones,
   Jesus, Jesus, Guide me through the dark night.

4. Jesus, Jesus, Savior of troubled man,
   Jesus, Jesus, Give me peace in my soul.

23 *Jesus the Only Thought of Thee*

Translated from St. Bernard

James Anthony Walsh

Je - sus the on - ly thought of Thee, With
sweet - ness fills my breast; But sweet - er
far thy face to see,
And on thy beau - ty feast.

2. Jesus, our hope when we repent,
Sweet source of all our grace,
Sole comfort in our banishment,
Oh, what, when face to face!

3. Thee, then, I'll seek, retired apart,
From world and business free;
When these shall knock, I'll shut my heart,
And keep it all for Thee.

24 *Only a Veil*

James Anthony Walsh

On - ly a veil be - tween me and Thee, Je -
sus my Lord! A veil of bread it ap -
pears to me, Yet seem - eth such that I
may not see Je - sus my God!

2. Lift not the veil between me and Thee,
Jesus, my Lord!
These eyes of earth can never see
The glory of your Divinity,
Jesus, my God.

3. Keep then the veil between me and Thee
Jesus, my Lord!
Some day 'twill fall when my soul is free
To gaze on Thee for eternity,
Jesus, my God.

25 *Praise Him*

Traditional

G
Bm
G
C
1. Praise ___ him, Praise ___ him; Praise him in the morn - ing;
C
Em
G
Praise him at the noon - time. Praise ___ him,
Bm
G
D7
G
Praise ___ him. Praise him when the sun goes down.

2. Love him 3. Serve him 4. Trust him 5. Thank him 6. Jesus

26 *Turn Your Eyes upon Jesus*

Words and music: Helen H. Lemmel

1. O soul, are you wea-ry and trou - bled? No light in the
2. Thru death in-to life ev-er - last - ing He passed, and we
3. His word shall not fail you— He prom - ised; Be-lieve Him, and
dark-ness you see? There's light for a look at the Sav - ior, And
fol-low Him there; O-ver us sin no more hath do-min - ion— For
all will be well: Then go to a world that is dy - ing, His
life more a-bun-dant and free!
more than con-q'rors we are!
per-fect sal-va-tion to tell!
CHORUS
Turn your eyes up-on Je - sus,
Look full in His won-der-ful face,
won-der-ful face,
And the things of
earth will grow strange-ly dim In the light of His glo-ry and grace.

27 *Lord Who Throughout These Forty Days*

St. Flavian, Claudia F. Hernaman, alt. — John Day's Psalter 1562

1. Lord who through - out these for - ty days For
2. As you with Sa - tan did con - tend And
1. us did fast and pray, Teach us with you to
2. did the vic - t'ry win, O give us strength in
mourn our sins, And close by you to stay.
you to fight, In you to con - quer sin.

3. As you did hunger and did thirst,
So teach us, gracious Lord,
To die to self and so to live
By your most holy word.

4. Abide with us, that through this life
Of suff'ring and of pain
An Easter of unending joy
We may at last attain.

28 *The Old Rugged Cross*

Words and music: George Bennard

1. On a hill far a - way stood an old rug - ged cross, The
2. Oh, the old rug - ged cross, so de - spised by the world, Has a
3. In the old rug - ged cross, stained with blood so di - vine, A
4. To the old rug - ged cross I will ev - er be true, Its
em - blem of suf-f'ring and shame; And I love that old cross where the
won-drous at - trac - tion for me; For the dear Lamb of God left His
won - drous beau - ty I see; For 'twas on that old cross Je - sus
shame and re - proach gladly bear; Then He'll call me some day to my
dear - est and best For a world of lost sin - ners was slain.
glo - ry a - bove To bear it to dark Cal - va - ry.
suf - fered and died To par - don and sanc - ti - fy me.
home far a - way, Where His glo - ry for - ev - er I'll share.
Chorus
So I'll cher - ish the old rug - ged cross, Till my
cross, the old rug - ged cross,

tro - phies at last I lay down; — I will cling to the old rug - ged
cross, the
cross, — And ex - change it some day for a crown. —
old rug - ged cross,

29 *Have Mercy on Me*

C. Uehlein

Have mer - cy on me, O God, have mer - cy! In

you — my soul — has tak - en ref - uge!

30 *All Glory, Laud, and Honor*

Theodulph of Orleans. Tr. by John M. Neale

Melchoir Teschner

Refrain
1. All glo - ry, laud, and hon - our To thee, Re - deem - er, King,
Fine
1. To whom the lips of chil - dren Made sweet ho - san - nas ring.
2. Thou art the King of Is - rael, Thou Da - vid's roy - al Son,
3. The com - pa - ny of an - gels Are prais - ing thee on high,
4. The peo ple of the He - brews With palms be - fore thee went;
D.C.
2. Who in the Lord's name com - est, The King and bles - sed One.
3. And mor - tal men and all __ things Cre - at - ed make re - ply.
4. Our praise and pray'r and an - thems Be - fore thee we pre - sent.

5. To thee before thy passion
   They sang their hymns of praise;
   To thee now high exalted
   Our melody we raise.

6. Thou didst accept their praises,
   Accept the pray'rs we bring,
   Who in all good delightest
   Thou good and gracious King.

31 *The Children of the Hebrews*

Liturgy, Palm Sunday

C. Uehlein

The chil - dren of the He - brews, bear - ing ol - ive
branch - es, went to meet the Lord, cry - ing out and

say - ing: "Ho - san - na in the high - est!"

Ballad of the Passion

For David Cronin + Vietnam 1968

C. Uehlein

Dm
Am
1. After the Pass-o-ver supper, Peter James and
John
Went to Geth-se-ma-ne with the Lord,
where he prayed a-lone:
"Fa-ther, if it be pos-si-ble,
Gm
take this cup from me!
But not my will but

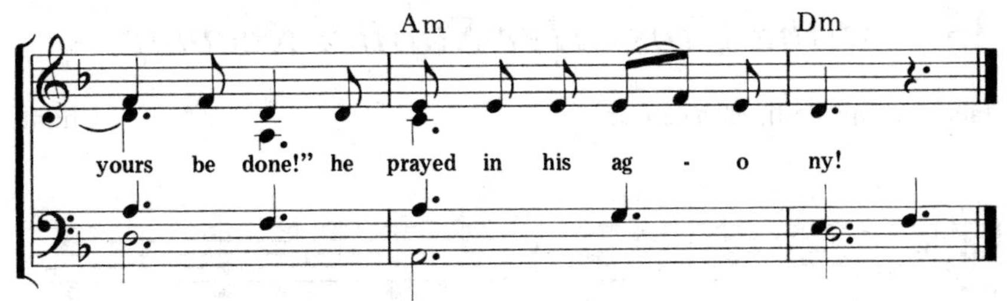
Am
Dm
yours be done!" he prayed in his ag - o ny!

2. Thirty pieces of silver the Temple elders paid
For the betrayal of Jesus by Judas, the renegade.
Pilate weakened and washed his hands when the people cried:
"Give us Barabbas! He's our man! But have Jesus crucified!"

3. Then Jesus felt the lashes sting him one by one!
Cloak of kingly purple clung to God the Son.
Crown of thorns upon his head, reed for royal mace,
"Long live the King of the Jews!" they yelled, and slapped him in the face!

4. Jesus, weak and trem-bling, shouldered his heavy load.
Out to the Skull-Place they led him, stumbling down the road.
There to the wood they nailed him, Pilate's soldier crew.
"Father," he prayed, "forgive them! They don't know what they do!"

5. People stood round and mocked him, saying, "Come down from the cross!"
Now it seemed that his whole life was a total loss.
"Father, why have you forsaken me?" Jesus loudly cried.
Then he breathed his last breath, and hung his head and died!

6. Jesus, Blessed Savior, make us always aware
Of your presence in all men; help us see you there!
When we turn from our neighbor or do him evil, then
We reject you all over and crucify you again!

33 *At the Cross Her Station Keeping*

Jacopone da Todi, 13th century

Chant

1. At the cross her sta - tion keep - ing, Stood the mourn - ful
2. Through her heart, his sor - row shar - ing, All his bit - ter
1. Mo - ther weep - ing, Close to Je - sus to the last.
2. an - guish bear - ing, Now at length the sword had passed.

3. O how sad and sore distressed
Was that Mother highly blessed
Of the sole begotten One!

4. Christ above in torment hangs,
She beneath beholds the pangs
Of her dying, glorious Son.

5. Is there one who would not weep,
'Whelmed in miseries so deep,
Christ's dear Mother to behold?

6. Holy Mother, pierce me through,
In my heart each wound renew
Of my Savior crucified.

7. Let me share with you his pain,
Who for all our sins was slain,
Who for me in torments died.

8. Let me to my latest breath,
In my body bear the death
Of that dying Son of yours.

34 *O Sacred Head*

St. Bernard — Hans Leo Hassler. Adapted by J.S. Bach

1. O sa - cred Head, sur - round - ed By crown of pierc - ing thorn.
2. In this thy bit - ter pas - sion, Good shep - herd, think _ of me
3. O Je - sus, we a - dore thee, Our thorn-crowned Lord and King.
1. O bleed - ing Head, so wound - ed, Re - viled, and put _ to scorn!
2. With thy most sweet com - pas - sion, Un - worth - y though _ I be:
3. We bow our hearts be - fore thee, And to thy Cross _ we cling.
Death's pal - lid hue comes o'er thee, The glow of life de - cays,
Be - neath _ thy Cross a - bid - ing For - ev - er would I rest,
O give _ us strength to bear it With pa - tience and with love,
Yet an - gel - hosts a - dore thee, And trem - ble as they gaze.
In thy _ dear love con - fid - ing, And with thy pre - sence blest.
That we _ may tru - ly mer - it A glo - rious crown a - bove.

35 *Were You There?*

Spiritual

1 Were you there when they cru - ci - fied my Lord? Were you
2 Were you there when they nailed him to the tree? Were you
3 Were you there when they laid him in the tomb? Were you
there when they cru - ci - fied my Lord?
there when they nailed him to the tree? Oh! . . . .
there when they laid him in the tomb?
Some-times it caus - es me to trem - ble, trem - ble, trem - ble.
Were you there when they cru - ci - fied my Lord?
Were you there when they nailed him to the tree?
Were you there when they laid him in the tomb?

36 *When I Survey the Wondrous Cross*

Isaac Watts

Arr. by Lowell Mason

1. When I sur - vey the won - drous cross
2. For - bid it, Lord, that I should boast
3. See, from His head, His hands, His feet,
4. Were the whole realm of na - ture mine,
On which the Prince of glo - ry died,
Save in the death of Christ, my Lord;
Sor - row and love flow min - gled down;
That were a pres - ent far too small:
My rich - est gain I count but loss,
All the vain things that charm me most,
Did e'er such love and sor - row meet,
Love so a - maz - ing, so di - vine,
And pour con - tempt on all my pride.
I sac - ri - fice them to His blood.
Or thorns com - pose so rich a crown?
De - mands my soul, my life, my all.

37 *At the Lamb's High Feast*

Jakob Hintze, 1678, alt. Harmony by J.S. Bach

1. At the Lamb's high feast we sing Praise to our vic - to - rious King,
2. Where the Pas - chal blood is poured, Death's dark an - gel sheathes his sword;
He has washed us in the tide Flow - ing from his o - pen side;
Is - rael's hosts tri - umph - ant go Through the wave that drowns the foe.
Praise we him, whose love di - vine Gives his sa - cred Blood for wine,
Praise we Christ, whose blood was shed, Pas - chal vic - tim, Pas - chal bread;
Gives his Bo - dy for the feast, Christ the vic - tim, Christ the priest.
With sin - cer - i - ty and love Eat we man - na from a - bove.

38 *Christ the Lord Is Ris'n Today*

Victimae Paschali Laudes | Traditional

1. Christ the Lord is ris'n to - day; Chris - tians, haste your vows to pay;
2. Christ, the Vic - tim un - de - filed, Man to God has rec - on - ciled;
3. Christ, who once for sin - ners bled, Now the first - born from the dead,
1. Of - fer you your prais - es meet At the Pas - chal_ Vic - tim's feet.
2. When in strange and aw - ful strife Met to - geth - er_ death and life;
3. Throned in end - less might and power, Lives and reigns for - ev - er - more.
1. For the sheep the Lamb has bled, Sin - less in the sin - ner's stead;
2. Chris - tians, on this hap - py day Haste with joy your vows to pay.
3. Hail, e - ter - nal Hope on high! Hail, our King of Vic - to - ry!
1. Christ, the Lord, is ris'n on high, Now he lives no_ more to die!
2. Christ, the Lord, is ris'n on high, Now he lives no_ more to die!
3. Hail, our Prince of life a - dored! Help and save us,_ gra - cious Lord.

39 *Be Joyful, Mary*

Regina Coeli, Jubila

Leisentritt's Gesangbuch

1. Be joy - ful, Mar - y, heav'n - ly Queen, be
2. The Son you bore by heav - en's grace, be
3. The Lord has ris - en from the dead, be
4. Then pray to God, O Vir - gin fair, be
1. joy - ful, Mar - y! Your grief is changed to
2. joy - ful, Mar - y! Did by his death our
3. joy - ful, Mar - y! He rose in glo - ry
4. joy - ful, Mar - y! That he our souls to
1. joy se - rene, al - le - lu -
2. guilt e - rase, al - le - lu -
3. as he said, al - le - lu -
4. heav - en bear, al - le - lu -

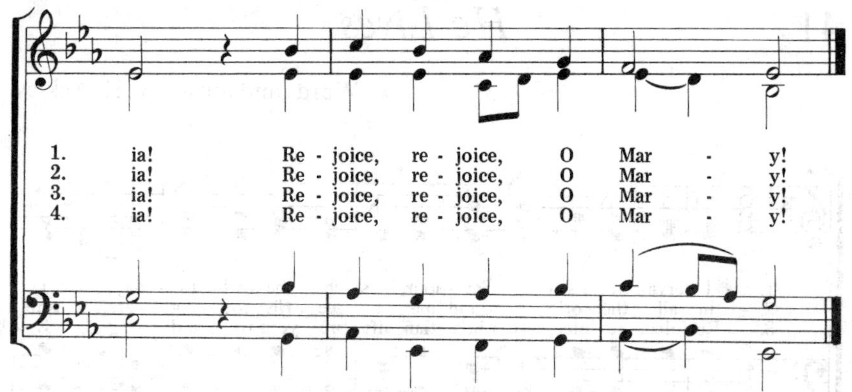

1. ia! Re - joice, re - joice, O Mar - y!
2. ia! Re - joice, re - joice, O Mar - y!
3. ia! Re - joice, re - joice, O Mar - y!
4. ia! Re - joice, re - joice, O Mar - y!

40 *Jesus Shall Reign*

Isaac Watts

John Hatton

1. Je - sus shall reign where e'er the__ sun Does his suc -
2. From north to south the__ prin - ces__ meet To pay their
3. To Him shall end - less__ pray'r be__ made, And end - less
4. Peo - ple and realms of__ ev - 'ry__ tongue, Dwell on His

ces - sive jour - neys run; His king - dom spread from
hom - age at His feet; While west - ern em - pires
prais - es crown His head; His name like sweet per -
love with sweet - est song, And in - fant voic - es

shore to shore, Till moons shall wax and wane no more.
own their Lord, And sav - age tribes at - tend His word.
fume shall rise With ev - 'ry morn - ing sac - ri - fice.
shall pro - claim Their ear - ly bless - ings on His name.

41

He Lives

Words and music: A. H. Ackley

1. I serve a ris - en Sav - iour, He's in the world to - day; I know that He is liv - ing, what - ev - er men may say; I see His hand of mer - cy, I hear His voice of cheer, And just the time I need Him He's al - ways near.
2. In all the world a - round me I see His lov - ing care, And tho' my heart grows wea - ry I nev - er will de - spair; I know that He is lead - ing, thru all the storm - y blast, The day of His ap - pear - ing will come at last.
3. Re - joice, re - joice, O Chris - tian, lift up your voice and sing E - ter - nal hal - le - lu - jahs to Je - sus Christ the King! The Hope of all who seek Him, the Help of all who find, None oth - er is so lov - ing, so good and kind.

Refrain Spirited
He lives, He lives, Christ Je - sus lives to - day! He
He lives, He lives,
walks with me and talks with me a - long life's nar - row way. He
lives, He lives, sal - va - tion to im - part! You
He lives, He lives,
rit.
ff
ask me how I know He lives? He lives with - in my heart.

42 *Jesus Christ Is Ris'n Today*

From Lyra Davidica

1. Je - sus Christ is ris'n to - day,
2. Hymns of praise then let us sing,
3. But the pains which he en - dured,
Al - - le - lu - ia!
1. Our tri - umph - ant ho - ly day,
2. Un - to Christ, our heav'n - ly King,
3. Our sal - va - tion have pro - cured;
Al - - le - lu - ia!
1. Who did once up - on the cross,
2. Who en - dured the cross and grave,
3. Now a - bove the sky he's King,
Al - - le - lu - ia!
1. Suf - fer to re - deem our loss.
2. Sin - ners to re - deem and save.
3. Where the an - gels ev - er sing.
Al - - le - lu - ia!

43 O Queen of Heaven

Regina Coeli

Chant

O Queen of Heav - en, be joy - ful, al - le - lu - ia,
For he, the Son whom you did bear for us, al - le - lu - ia,
Is now ris - en as he fore - told, al - le - lu - ia.
Pray for us to the Fath - er, al - le - lu - ia.

44 *Praise, My Soul*

Lauda Anima

John Goss, 1869

1. Praise, my soul, the King of heav - en; To his
2. Praise him for his grace and fa - vor To our
3. Fa - ther - like he tends and spares us; Well our
4. An - gels, help us to a - dore him; You be -
1. feet thy trib - ute bring; Ran - somed, healed, re - stored, for -
2. fa - thers in dis - tress; Praise him still the same as
3. fee - ble frame he knows; In his hand he gen - tly
4. hold him face to face; Sun and moon, bow down be -
1. giv - en, Ev - er - more his prais - es sing: Al - le - lu - ia!
2. ev - er, Slow to chide and swift to bless: Al - le - lu - ia!
3. bears us, Res - cues us from all our foes. Al - le - lu - ia!
4. fore him, Dwell - ers all in time and space. Al - le - lu - ia!
1. Al - le - lu - ia! Praise the ev - er - last - ing King.
2. Al - le - lu - ia! Glo - rious in his faith - ful - ness.
3. Al - le - lu - ia! Wide - ly yet his mer - cy flows.
4. Al - le - lu - ia! Praise with us the God of grace.

45

The Strife Is O'er

G.P. Sante Da Palestrina, 1588. Adapted, William H. Monk, 1861

Al - le - lu - ia! Al - le - lu - ia! Al - le - lu - ia!
1. The strife is o'er, the bat - tle done, The vic - to - ry of life is won; The song of triumph has be - gun. Al - le - lu - ia!
2. The powers of death have done their worst, But Christ their le - gions hath dis - persed: Let shout of ho - ly joy out burst. Al - le - lu - ia!
3. The three sad days are quick - ly sped, He ri - ses glo - rious from the dead: All glo - ry to our ris - en Head! Al - le - lu - ia!

46 *Breathe on Me, Breath of God*

Edwin Hatch — Robert Jackson

1. Breathe on me, Breath of God, Fill me with life a new, That I may
2. Breathe on me, Breath of God, Un - til my heart is pure, Un - til with
3. Breathe on me, Breath of God, Till I am whol - ly Thine, Un - til this
4. Breathe on me, Breath of God, So shall I nev - er die, But live with

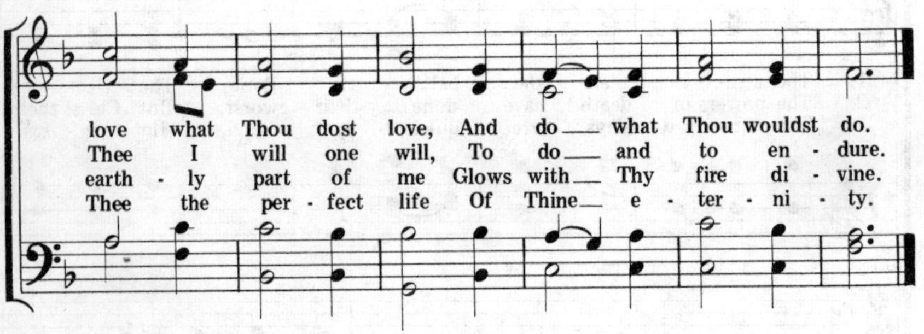
love what Thou dost love, And do what Thou wouldst do.
Thee I will one will, To do and to en - dure.
earth - ly part of me Glows with Thy fire di - vine.
Thee the per - fect life Of Thine e - ter - ni - ty.

V. The charity of God is poured forth in our hearts.
R. By his Spirit dwelling in us.

Let us pray. Almighty and eternal God, who in your kindness gave us a new birth through water and the Holy Spirit, send forth from heaven upon us your sevenfold Spirit, the Holy Consoler. Amen.

Come, Holy Ghost

Tr. F. Caswall, 1849, alt.

L. Lambillotte, S.J., 1843

1. Come, Ho - ly Ghost, Cre - a - tor blest, And in our
2. O Com - fort - er, to thee we cry, Thou heav'n - ly
3. Praise be to thee, Fa - ther and Son, And Ho - ly
1. hearts take up thy rest; Come with thy grace
2. gift of God most high, Thou font of life
3. Spir - it, with them one; And may the Son
1. and heav'n - ly aid To fill the hearts which thou hast
2. and fire of love, And sweet a - noint - ing from a -
3. on us be - stow The gifts that from the Spir - it
1. made. To fill the hearts which thou hast made.
2. bove. And sweet a - noint - ing from a - bove.
3. flow. The gifts that from the Spir - it flow.

48 *Pentecostal Power*

Charlotte G. Homer

Charles H. Gabriel

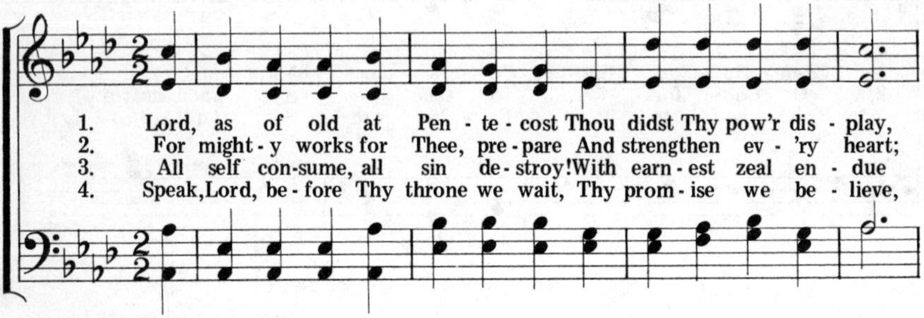

1. Lord, as of old at Pen - te - cost Thou didst Thy pow'r dis - play,
2. For might - y works for Thee, pre - pare And strengthen ev - 'ry heart;
3. All self con-sume, all sin de - stroy! With earn - est zeal en - due
4. Speak, Lord, be - fore Thy throne we wait, Thy prom - ise we be - lieve,

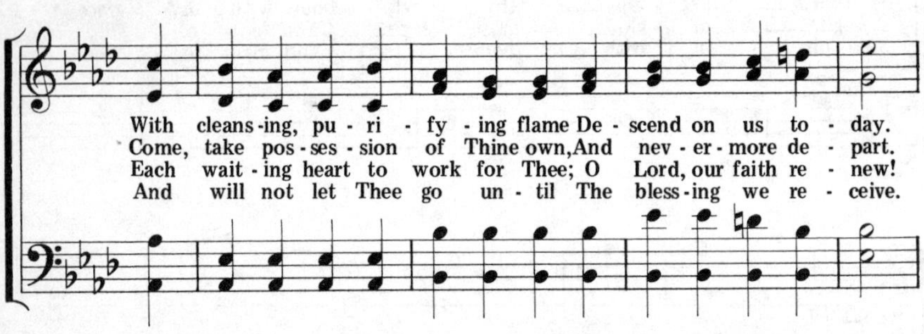

With cleans-ing, pu - ri - fy - ing flame De - scend on us to - day.
Come, take pos - ses - sion of Thine own, And nev - er - more de - part.
Each wait - ing heart to work for Thee; O Lord, our faith re - new!
And will not let Thee go un - til The bless-ing we re - ceive.

Chorus

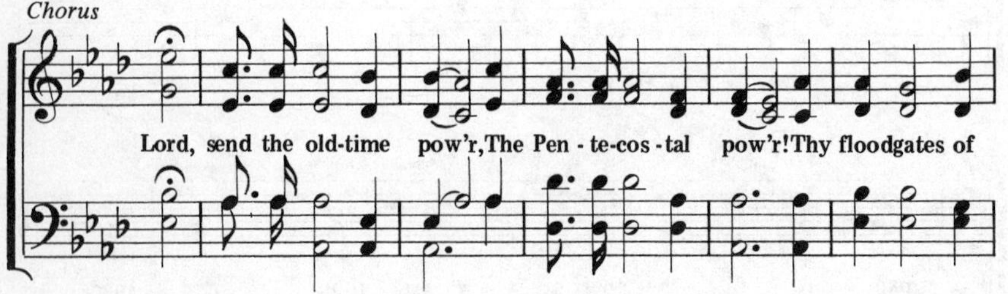
Lord, send the old-time pow'r, The Pen - te-cos - tal pow'r! Thy floodgates of

bless - ing on us throw o - pen wide! Lord, send the old time pow'r, the

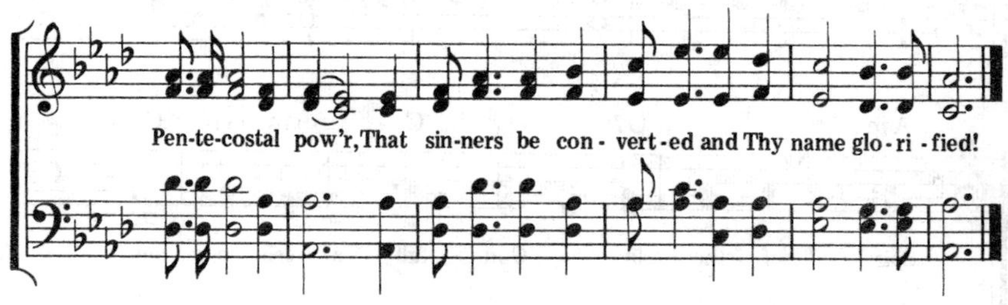
Pen-te-costal pow'r, That sin-ners be con - vert - ed and Thy name glo - ri - fied!

Prayer to the Holy Spirit

Come, Holy Spirit, fill the hearts of the faithful, and kindle in them the fire of your love.

V. Send forth your Spirit, and they shall be created.

R. You shall renew the face of the earth.

Let us pray. O God, you have instructed the hearts of the faithful by the light of the Holy Spirit. Grant that through the same Holy Spirit we may be truly wise and always rejoice in his consolation. Through Christ our Lord. Amen.

49 *Spirit of the Living God*

Capo = 3

Daniel Iverson

C G7 C Am G7 C
Spir - it of the liv - ing God, fall a - fresh on me.
Am G7 C Am G7 C
Spir - it of the liv - ing God, fall a - fresh on me.
G7 C D7 G C7
Melt me, mold me, fill me, use me.
C G7 C Am G7 C
Spir - it of the liv - ing God, fall a - fresh on me.

Repeat, using "us" instead of "me" the second time.

Spirit of Truth and Light

C. Uehlein

Gm
Cm
Gm
Cm
1. Spir-it of truth — and light,
Give us your love with-out
Gm
Cm
Gm
end.
And to our rest - less hearts,
Dm
Gm
de capo
fine
peace ev - er - last - ing send.

2. Though Christ was Lord divine,
He did not cling to his state,
But emptied out himself
To share our lowly fate!

3. Humbling himself as man,
He became more humble still;
Death on the cross he bore,
Doing his Father's will!

4. So God has raised him on high
And gave him such a name
That truly does surpass
All other titles' claim!

5. Therefore all creatures above,
Those here on earth and below,
Should bend the knee at that
name,
Worship and praise to show!

6. Let ev'ry tongue proclaim;
"Jesus is risen King!"
"Glory!" to Father and Son
And to the Spirit sing!

51 *God Father, Praise and Glory*

Mainz Gesangbuch, 1833

1. God Fa - ther, praise and glo - ry Thy chil - dren bring to thee. Thy
2. And thou, Lord co - e - ter - nal, God's sole_ be - got - ten Son. O
3. O Ho - ly Ghost, Cre - a - tor, Thou gift_ of God most high Life
1. grace and peace to man kind Shall now_ for - ev - er be.
2. Je - sus, King a - noint - ed Who have_ re - demp - tion won.
3. love and ho - ly wis - dom Our weak - ness now sup - ply.
Refrain
O most ho - ly Trin - i - ty, Un - di - vid - ed_ U - ni - ty.
Ho - ly God, Might - y God, God Im - mor - tal, be a - dored.

52 *Holy, Holy, Holy! Lord God Almighty!*

Nicaea — John B. Dykes, 1861

1. Ho - ly, ho - ly, ho - ly! Lord God Al - might - y!
2. Ho - ly, ho - ly, ho - ly! All the saints a - dore thee,
3. Ho - ly, ho - ly, ho - ly! Though the dark - ness hide thee,
4. Ho - ly, ho - ly, ho - ly! Lord God Al - might - y!
1. Ear - ly in the morn - ing our song shall rise to thee:
2. Cast - ing down their gold - en crowns a - round the glass - y sea;
3. Though the eye of sin - ful man thy glo - ry may not see;
4. All thy works shall praise thy name in earth, and sky, and sea;
1. Ho - ly, ho - ly, ho - ly! Mer - ci - ful and might - y,
2. Cher - u - bim and ser - a - phim fall - ing down be - fore thee,
3. On - ly thou art ho - ly! there is none be - side thee,
4. Ho - ly, ho - ly, ho - ly! Mer - ci - ful and might - y,
1. God in three per - sons, bless - ed Trin - i - ty.
2. Which wert, and art, and ev - er - more shall be.
3. Per - fect in power, in love, and pu - ri - ty.
4. God in three per - sons, bless - ed Trin - i - ty.

53 *On This Day*

LeMans Breviary Freylinghausen's Gesangbuch, 1704

1. On this day, the first of days,
2. On this day th'e - ter - nal Son
3. Fa - ther, who didst fash - ion man
4. Word - made - flesh, all hail to thee!
5. Ho - ly Spir - it, you im - part
6. God, the bless - ed Three in One,
1. God the Fa - ther's name we praise; Who, cre - a - tion's
2. O - ver death his tri - umph won; On this day the
3. God - like in thy lov - ing plan, Fill us with that
4. Thou from sin hast set us free; And with thee we
5. Gifts of love to ev - 'ry heart; Give us Light and
6. May thy ho - ly will be done; In thy word our
1. Lord and Spring, Did the world from dark - ness bring.
2. Spir - it came With his gifts of liv - ing flame.
3. love di - vine, And con - form our wills to thine.
4. die and rise Un - to God in sac - ri - fice.
5. Grace, we pray, Fill our hearts this ho - ly day.
6. souls are free, And we rest this day with thee.

Praise God from Whom All Blessings Flow

Thomas Ken

Louis Bourgeois

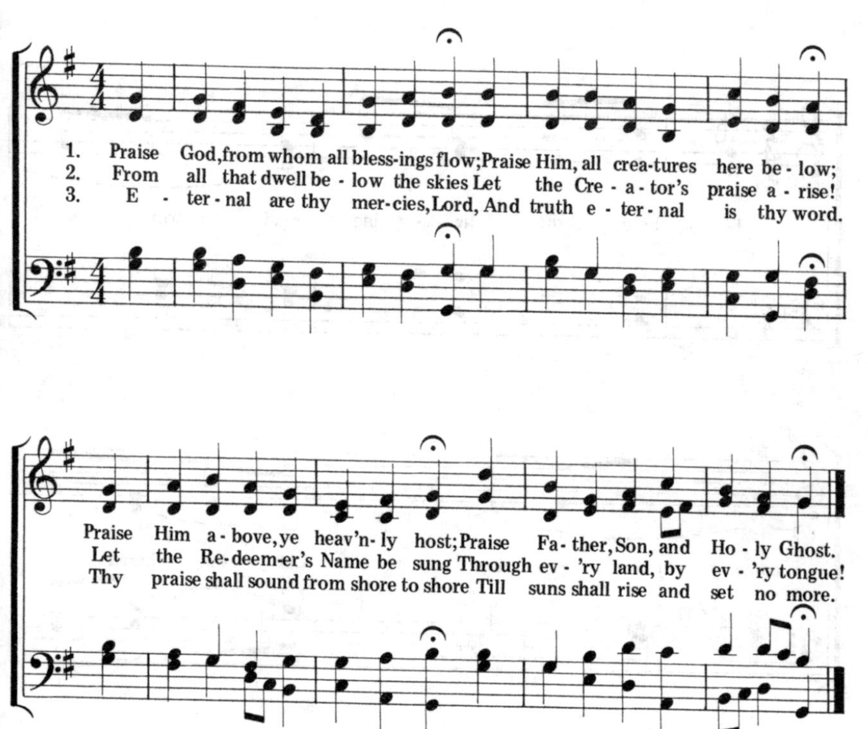
1. Praise God, from whom all bless-ings flow; Praise Him, all crea-tures here be - low;
2. From all that dwell be - low the skies Let the Cre - a - tor's praise a - rise!
3. E - ter - nal are thy mer-cies, Lord, And truth e - ter - nal is thy word.
Praise Him a - bove, ye heav'n - ly host; Praise Fa - ther, Son, and Ho - ly Ghost.
Let the Re-deem-er's Name be sung Through ev - 'ry land, by ev - 'ry tongue!
Thy praise shall sound from shore to shore Till suns shall rise and set no more.

55 *Behold the Living Bread*

Body and Blood of Christ

C. Uehlein

Be - hold the liv - ing Bread which has
come from a - bove! Eat this bread of
Life and live for - ev - er with God!

56

Learn of Me

Sacred Heart of Jesus

C. Uehlein

And_ Je - sus said: Learn of me, for I am

gen - tle and low - ly of heart.

57 *Crown Him with Many Crowns*

Matthew Bridges

George J. Elvey

1. Crown Him with man - y crowns, The Lamb up - on His throne;
2. Crown Him the Lord of life! Who tri-umphed o'er the grave;
3. Crown Him the Lord of heaven! One with the Fa - ther known,
Hark! how the heaven-ly an - them drowns All mu - sic but its own!
Who rose vic - to - rious to the strife For those He came to save:
One with the Spir - it through Him given From yon - der glo - rious throne!
A - wake, my soul, and sing Of Him who died for thee;
His glo - ries now we sing, Who died and rose on high;
To Thee be end - less praise, For Thou for us hast died;
And hail Him as thy match - less King Thro' all e - ter - ni - ty.
Who died e - ter - nal life to bring, And lives that death may die.
Be Thou, O Lord, through end - less days A - dored and mag - ni - fied.

58 *To Jesus Christ, Our Sov'reign King*

Msgr. Martin B. Hellriegel

Mainz Gesangbuch, 1870

To Je - sus Christ, our sov' - reign King, Who is the world's sal - va - tion, All praise and hom - age do we bring And thanks and ad - o - ra - tion.
Your reign ex - tend, O King be - nign, To ev - 'ry land and na - tion; For in your king - dom, Lord di - vine, A - lone we find sal - va - tion.
To you and to your Church, great King, We pledge our hearts' ob - la - tion; Un - til be - fore your throne we sing In end - less ju - bi - la - tion.
Refrain
Christ Je - sus, Vic - tor! Christ Je - sus, Rul - er! Christ Je - sus, Lord and Re - deem - er!

Text used by permission of author.

59 *Glorious God*

Sebastian Temple. Accomp. Jack Arden

Verses
Bb (A)
Eb (D)
Bb (A)
1. Glo - ri - ous God, King of cre - a - tion, We
2. Glo - ri - ous God, mag - ni - fi - cent, ho - ly, We
Eb (D)
Bb (A)
Eb (D)
F7 (E7)
1. praise you, We bless you, We wor - ship you in song:
2. love you, a - dore you, And come to you in prayer.
Bb (A)
Eb (D)
Bb (A)
1. Glo - ri - ous God, in ad - o - ra - tion.
2. Glo - ri - ous God, migh - ty e - ter - nal, We
F7 (E7)
Bb (A)
1. At your feet we be - long.
2. sing your praise ev - 'ry - where.
Fine

Refrain
F7(E7)
B♭(A)
Lord of life, Fa - ther al - might - y,
F7(E7)
B♭(A)
Lord of hearts, Christ the King.
F7(E7)
B♭(A)
Lord of love, Ho - ly Spir - it. To
C7(B7)
F7(E7)
whom we hom - age bring.
D.C.

60 Great Is the Lord

Mission Song

Isaiah
S. Suzanne Toolan
Refrain
Great is the Lord, wor-thy of praise, tell all the na-tions God is King!
Spread the news of his love!
1. The spir-it of the Lord is up-
2. How beau-ti-ful up-on the
3. Give glo-ry to the
1. on me be-cause the Lord has a-noint-ed me. He has
2. moun-tains, the feet of him who brings glad ti-dings, an-nounc-ing
3. Fa-ther, the Son and Ho-ly Spir-it blest, the God who
Fine
1. sent me to bring glad ti-dings to the low-ly, to the low-ly.
2. peace, bear-ing good news that the Lord God, he is King!
3. is, who was, who will be, for-ev-er, A-men.

61 *Holy God, We Praise Thy Name*

Te Deum

Vienna c. 1744

1. Ho - ly God, — we praise — thy Name; Lord of all, — we
2. Hark! the loud — ce - les - tial hymn An - gel choirs — a -
1. bow be - fore thee; All on earth — thy scep - ter claim,
2. bove are rais - ing; Cher - u - bim — and Ser - a - phim
1. All in heav - en a - bove — a - dore thee; In - fi - nite, — thy
2. In un - ceas - ing chor - us prais - ing; Fill the — heav'ns — with
1. vast do - main, Ev - er - last - ing is — thy reign.
2. sweet ac - cord: Ho - ly, ho - ly, ho - ly, Lord!

62 *Now Thank We All Our God*

Martin Rinkart
Catherine Winkworth

Crüger's Praxis Pietatis, Melica

1. Now thank we all our God With heart and hands and voic - es,
2. O may this boun-teous God Thru all our life be near us,
3. All praise and thanks to God The Fa - ther now be giv - en,
Who won-drous things hath done, In whom His world re - joic - es;
With ev - er joy - ful hearts And bless - ed peace to cheer us;
The Son, and Him who reigns With them in high-est heav - en;
Who, from our moth-ers' arms Hath blessed us on our way
And keep us in His grace, And guide us when per - plexed,
The one e - ter - nal God Whom earth and heav'n a - dore;
With count-less gifts of love, And still is ours to - day.
And free us from all ills In this world and the next.
For thus it was, is now, And shall be ev - er - more.

63 O Lord, We Bless You

C. Uehlein

1. O Lord, we bless you for the glo - ry of your
1. Be - ing! You fill our hearts with won - der and with awe!
1. Your knowledge and your might are be - yond our com - pre - hen - sion,
1. but by your grace we know your love, your law!
1-3.
4. organ
law!
*

* This variation in final cadence affects only the accompaniment.

2. O Lord, we thank you for the beauty of creation,
The vast expanse of all the universe,
For ev'ry creature that reflects your perfect goodness,
All things that you in time and space disperse!

3. But most of all, Lord, thank you for your incarnation,
For being born into our here and now
To die and rise again in your glorious resurrection,
That with your life our own you might endow!

4. And now we pray, Lord, put an end to our divisions!
Let us give witness to you, Lord of all.
Strengthen in unity all who bear the name of Christian
To keep us true to your loving call!

64 *Praise Him! Praise Him!*

Fanny J. Crosby

Chester G. Allen

1. Praise Him! praise Him! Je - sus, our bless - ed Re - deem - er!
2. Praise Him! praise Him! Je - sus, our bless - ed Re - deem - er!
3. Praise Him! praise Him! Je - sus, our bless - ed Re - deem - er!
Sing, O Earth, His won - der ful love pro - claim! Hail Him!
For our sins He suf - fered, and bled, and died; He our
Heav'n - ly por - tals loud with ho - san - nas ring! Je - sus,
hail Him! high - est arch - an - gels in glo - ry; Strength and hon - or
Rock, our hope of e - ter - nal sal - va - tion, Hail Him! hail Him!
Sav - ior, reign - eth for - ev - er and ev - er; Crown Him! crown Him!

give to His ho - ly name! Like a shep - herd, Je - sus will guard His
Je - sus the Cru - ci - fied. Sound His Praises! Je - sus who bore our
Pro - phet, and Priest, and King! Christ is com - ing! o - ver the world vic-
chil - dren, In His arms He car - ries them all day long:
sor - rows, Love un - bound - ed, won - der - ful, deep and strong:
to - rious, Pow'r and glo - ry un - to the Lord be - long:
Refrain
Praise Him! praise Him! tell of His ex - cel - lent great - ness;
Praise Him! praise Him! ev - er in joy - ful song!

65 *Praise to the Holiest*

John Henry Newman

Richard R. Terry, 1912

1. Praise to the Ho - liest in the height, And in the depth be praise, In all his words most won - der - ful, Most sure in all his ways.
2. O lov - ing wis - dom of our God! When all was sin and shame, A sec - ond Ad - am to the fight And to the res - cue came.
3. O wis - est love! that flesh and blood Which did in Ad - am fail, Should strive a fresh a - gainst their foe, Should strive and should pre - vail.

66 *Praise to the Lord, the Almighty*

Joachim Neander, 1680

Stralsund Gesangbuch, 1665

1. Praise to the Lord, the Al-might-y, the King of cre-a-tion; O my soul, praise him, for he is thy health and sal-va-tion. All ye who hear, Now to his al-tar draw near, Join-ing in glad ad-o-ra-tion.
2. Praise to the Lord, who doth pros-per thy work and de-fend thee; Sure-ly his good-ness and mer-cy here dai-ly at-tend thee. Pon-der a-new What the Al-might-y can do, If with his love he be-friend thee.

67 *To God Be the Glory*

Fanny J. Crosby

William H. Doane

Ab Eb Ab Eb Ab
1. To God be the glo - ry, great things He hath done; So
2. O per - fect re - demp - tion, the pur - chase of blood, To
3. Great things He has taught us, great things He hath done, And
Db Ab Bb Eb
loved He the world that He gave us His Son, Who
ev - 'ry be - liev - er the prom - ise of God; The
great our re - joic - ing thro' Je - sus the Son; But
Ab Eb Ab Eb Ab Ab7
yield - ed His life an a - tone - ment for sin, And
vil - est of - fend - er who tru - ly be - lieves, That
pur - er, and high - er, and great - er will be Our
Db Ab/Eb Eb Ab
o - pened the life - gate that all may go in.
mo - ment from Je - sus a par - don re - ceives.
won - der, our trans - port, when Je - sus we see.

Refrain
Ab
Ab Eb Ab
Praise the Lord, praise the Lord, Let the earth hear His
Eb Eb7 Ab Eb
voice! Praise the Lord, praise the Lord, Let the peo - ple re -
Ab Eb Ab Eb
joice! O come to the Fa - ther, thro' Je - sus the
Ab Db Ab/Eb Eb7 Ab
Son, And give Him the glo - ry, great things He hath done.

68 *Faith of Our Fathers*

Frederick W. Faber

H. F. Hemy

1. Faith of our fa - thers! liv - ing still In spite of dun-geon, fire___ and sword, O how our hearts___ beat high___ with joy When-e'er we hear that glo - rious word! Faith of our fa - thers! ho - ly faith! We will be true to thee till death!
2. Our fa - thers, chained in pris - ons dark, Were still in heart and con - science free: How sweet would be___ their chil - dren's fate, If they, like them, could die___ for thee! Faith of our fa - thers! ho - ly faith! We will be true to thee till death!
3. Faith of our fa - thers! we___ will love Both friend and foe in all___ our strife: And preach thee, too,___ as love___ knows how, By kind - ly words and vir - tuous life: Faith of our fa - thers! ho - ly faith! We will be true to thee till death!

69 *The Church's One Foundation*

Samuel J. Stone — Samuel S. Wesley

1. The Church's one foun - da - tion Is Je - sus Christ her Lord;
2. E - lect from ev - ery na - tion Yet one o'er all the earth,
3. 'Mid toil and tri - bu la - tion And tu - mult of her war,
4. Yet she on earth has u - nion With God the Three in One,

1. She is his new cre - a - tion By wa - ter and the Word:
2. Her char - ter of sal - va - tion One Lord, one faith, one birth,
3. She waits the con - sum - ma - tion Of peace for ev - er - more;
4. And mys - tic sweet com - mu - nion With those whose rest is won:

1. From heav'n he came and sought her To be his ho - ly bride;
2. One ho - ly name she bless - es, Par - takes one ho - ly food,
3. Till with the vi - sion glo - rious Her long - ing eyes are blest,
4. O hap - py ones and ho - ly! Lord, give us grace that we,

1. With his own blood he bought her, And for her life he died.
2. And to one hope she press - es With ev - 'ry grace en - dued.
3. And the great Church vic - to - rious Shall be the Church at rest.
4. Like them, the meek and low - ly, On high may dwell with thee.

70 Hail Mary

Luke 1:28, 42 and Tradition

C. Uehlein

In a moderate, flowing tempo
Hail
GT.
SW.
ped.
Ma - ry full of grace the Lord is with you.
SW.
Bless - ed are __ you a - mong all wo - men
and

blessed is the fruit of your womb Je - sus.
In strict time
GT.
Ho - ly Ma - ry moth - er of
SW.

God
Pray for us
sin - ners
now and at the
hour of our death.
A - - -
men.
GT.

Hail, Holy Queen

Traditional

1. Hail,— ho - ly Queen en - throned a - bove, O Ma - ri - a!
2. Our— life, our sweet-ness here be - low, O Ma - ri - a!
1. Hail, moth - er of mer - cy and of love, O Ma - ri - a!
2. Our— hope— in sor - row and in woe, O Ma - ri - a!
Refrain
Tri - umph, all ye— che - ru - bim, Sing with us, ye— se - ra - phim,
Heav'n and earth re - sound the hymn: Sal - ve, sal - ve, sal - ve Re - gi - na!

72 Immaculate Mary

Lourdes Hymn

Traditional

1. Im - mac - u - late Mar - y, your prais - es we
2. In heav - en the bless - ed your glo - ry pro -
3. We pray for the Church, our true Moth - er on
1. sing. You reign now in splen - dor with Je - sus our King.
2. claim, On earth we your chil - dren in - voke your sweet name.
3. earth, And bless, Ho - ly Mar - y, the land of our birth.
Refrain
A - ve, A - ve, A - ve, Ma - ri - a!
A - ve, A - ve, Ma - ri - - a!

73 *Indian Magnificat*

Sr. M. Jorita

Refrain
Drum x x x x x x x x x Mag - ni - fi - cat
a - ni - ma me - a, Your heart was o - ver - flow - ing,
Vir - go Ma - ri - a, Vir - go Ma - ri - a O Ma - dre
mi - a, I sing with you Mag - ni - fi - cat a - ni - ma me - a.
Fine
1. The an - gel of the Lord ap - peared to you
2. And then un - to E - liz - a - beth you went
3. And so it was that God was born in you
1,2,3 Al - le - lu - ia!
1. Your an - swer to your God was, "Yes, I do."
2. And it is told a help - ing hand you lent.
3. Was born in you the Fa - ther's will to do.
Al - le - lu - ia! Fi - at, fi - at, be it done to me.
Moth - er, dear - est Moth - er, let me sing my song with you.
D.C.

This is best sung a capella with bongo drums for accompaniment

74 *Mary's Joy*

C. Uehlein

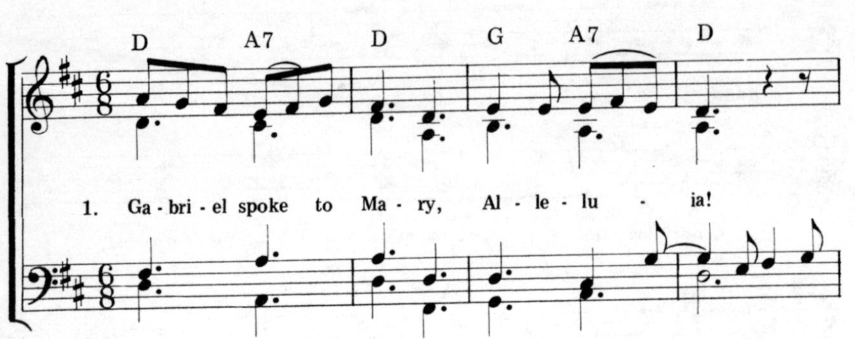
D
A7
D
G
A7
D
1. Ga - bri - el spoke to Ma - ry, Al - le - lu - ia!

A7
D
G
A7
D
"Soon in your womb you will car - ry," Al - le - lu - ia,

G
D
A7
"One who rules for e - ter - ni - ty," Al - le - lu - ia!

D
A7
D
G
A7
D
Ma - ry re - plied: "Be it done to me," Al - le - lu - ia!

2. Mary went off to the hill country, alleluia!
   Visited 'Lisabeth happily, alleluia!
   "Praise the Lord, O my soul," she sang, alleluia
   And her song through the ages rang, alleluia!

3. Mary gave birth in Bethlehem, alleluia,
   To the Savior of all men, alleluia!
   She is Virgin and Mother, alleluia!
   He is the God-man, our Brother, alleluia!

4. Up to the temple went Mary, alleluia!
   There she presented her baby, alleluia!
   Simeon's hope was fulfilled that day, alleluia!
   Anna stepped forth and had much to say, alleluia!

5. Jesus was not even in his teens, alleluia,
   When he was teaching the temple deans, alleluia.
   Mary and Joseph found him, alleluia,
   With all the teachers around him, alleluia!

6. Glory be to the Father, alleluia!
   Glory be to his only Son, alleluia!
   Glory be to the Spirit, alleluia!
   Glory be to the Three-in-One, alleluia!

75 *Mother of the Americas*

Charles G. Ruess

Our La - dy of Guad - a - lu - pe came to tell the new world of an
Our La - dy chose cen - tral Tep - e - yac to show this hem - i - sphere that
an - cient love. A mer - ci - ful moth - er she would be to
all were dear. And gave as a proof a price - less gift: her
Juan Di - e - go and all who heed her call. Dear
love - li - ness im - pressed on til - ma blest. Dear
Refrain
moth - er of the A - mer - i - cas. You prom - ised

hap - pi - ness. We thank you for your
care, your love - ly por - trait rare,
And beg that love which claimed our na - tions
from the start may ev - er claim our heart.

76 Sing of Mary

Anon. Plymouth Collection

1. Sing of Mar - y, pure and low - ly, Vir - gin
2. Sing of Je - sus, son of Mar - y, In the
3. Glo - ry be to God the Fa - ther, Glo - ry

1. moth - er un - de - filed, Sing of God's own
2. home at Na - za - reth. Toil and la - bor
3. be to God the Son; Glo - ry be to

1. Son most ho - ly, Who be - came her lit - tle child.
2. can - not wea - ry Love en - dur - ing un - to death.
3. God the Spir - it, Glo - ry to the Three in One.

1. Fair - est child of fair - est moth - er, God, the
2. Con - stant was the love he gave her, Though he
3. From the heart of bless - ed Mar - y, From all

1. Lord, who came to earth, Word - made - flesh, our
2. went forth from her side, Forth to preach and
3. saints the song as - cends, And the Church the

1. ver - y broth - er, Takes our na - ture by his birth.
2. heal and suf - fer, Till on Cal - va - ry he died.
3. strain re - ech - oes Un - to earth's re - mot - est ends.

77 *O Virgin Most Wise*

Liturgy, August 15 C. Uehlein

O Vir - gin most wise, where are you go - ing,
splen - did as the dawn? O
daugh - ter of Si - on, fair as the moon,
love - ly as the sun!

78 The Saints Proclaim God's Power

C. Uehlein

The saints pro - claim the pow'r and love of
God! They live now in end - less peace and
joy! They drank of the chal - ice of the
Lord and be - came the friends of ___ God!

79 *O Workman Worthy*

Roman Breviary
Tr. Christopher Rengers, OFMCap

Lawrence Cain

1. O work - man ___ wor - thy of all praise, So
2. Ser - ene you ___ know a roy - al line, Yet
3. O work - er, ___ eve - ry work - er's guide, You
4. O God, three - fold, yet ev - er one, Pa -

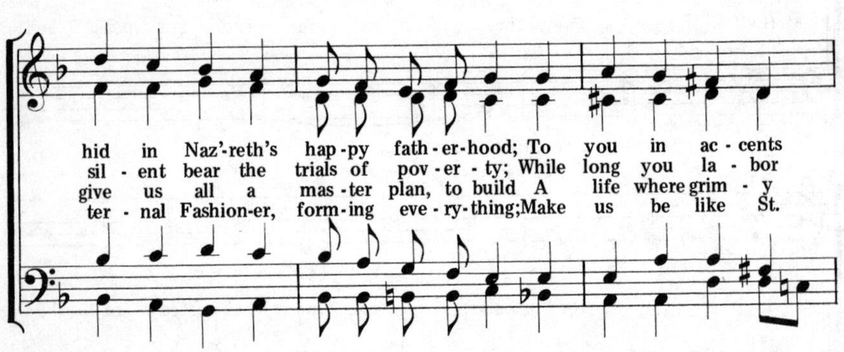
hid in Naz'-reth's hap-py fath-er-hood; To you in ac-cents
sil - ent bear the trials of pov-er-ty; While long you la - bor
give us all a mas-ter plan, to build A life where grim - y
ter - nal Fashion-er, form-ing eve-ry-thing; Make us be like St.

loud and full Our ___ hearts O Jo - seph, ___ now we raise.
with your hands, Pro - vid - ing for ___ home's ___ ho - ly shrine.
toil it - self And ___ work-shops may ___ be ___ sanc - ti - fied.
Jo - seph now, And ___ when at last ___ life's ___ course is run.

Chorus
Please help the poor, those in des - pair; Com -
pose un - ru - ly hearts and end all strife, So
that the Mys - tic Christ may grow Be -
neath your lov - ing fa - ther's care.

80 *Canticle of the Gift*

Refrain: Pat Uhl
Verses: Michael Gilligan

Pat Uhl

O WHAT A GIFT, WHAT A WON–DER – FUL GIFT; WHO CAN
TELL THE WON–DERS OF THE LORD? LET US O – PEN OUR EYES, OUR
EARS, AND OUR HEARTS; IT IS CHRIST THE LORD, IT IS HE!
1. In the still - ness of the night, when the world was a- sleep, the
Lord made his mes-sage known. It was then that his Word came
down from on high, from the Fa - ther's ro - yal ___ throne:
Christ our Lord and our King.
O WHAT A GIFT. . .

2. His might - y Word cuts quick and clean, far sharp - er than a two-edged
sword: O - pen your eyes, your ears, and your hearts, and
hear the Word of the Lord: Christ our Lord and our King. O WHAT A GIFT
3. He came to his peo - ple, the cho - sen race, that his
Fa - ther's will would be known; Li - on of Ju - dah,
Light of the World, our Re - deem - er came to his own:
Christ our Lord and our King. O WHAT A GIFT......
4. He lived here a - mong us, he worked here a - mong us,
morn - ing, night, and day; Showed us his glo - ry,

gave us a prom - ise, and then we turned a - way:
Christ our Lord and our King. O WHAT A GIFT. . . . .
5. At the Pass - o - ver meal on the night be - fore he died, he
lift - ed up his eyes and prayed. Then he broke the bread,
then he shared the wine. . . . the gift that God had
made: Christ our Lord and our King. O WHAT A GIFT. . . . . .
6. On the hill of Cal - va - ry, the world held its breath; and
there for the world to see, the Fa - ther gave his Son, his

ver - y own Son for the love of you and me:
Christ our Lord and our King. O WHAT A GIFT......
7. Ear - ly on that morn - ing when the guards were sleep - ing, the
Fa - ther re - vealed his might; Christ in his glo - ry a -
rose from the dead, the Lord of Life and Light:
Christ our Lord and our King. O WHAT A GIFT.......
8. On the road to Em-may - us, the glo - ry that is his, the dis -
ci - ples could nev - er see. Then he broke the bread,

then he shared the wine; it is the Lord, it is he:
Christ our Lord and our King. O WHAT A GIFT......
9. Now look a - round you and o - pen your eyes; re -
mem-ber the Spir - it is here. Here with - in his Church, his
peo-ple are one. Look, the Lord is near: Christ our Lord and our
King. O WHAT A GIFT, WHAT A WON—DER—FUL GIFT; WHO CAN
TELL THE WON—DERS OF THE LORD? LET US O—PEN OUR EYES, OUR
EARS, AND OUR HEARTS; IT IS CHRIST THE LORD, IT IS HE!

81 *Christians, Let Us Love One Another*

Vs. 1 Fr. A. Nigro, S.J.
Vss. 2, 3, 5, 6, Sr. Claudia Foltz
Vs. 4 Anon.

Traditional

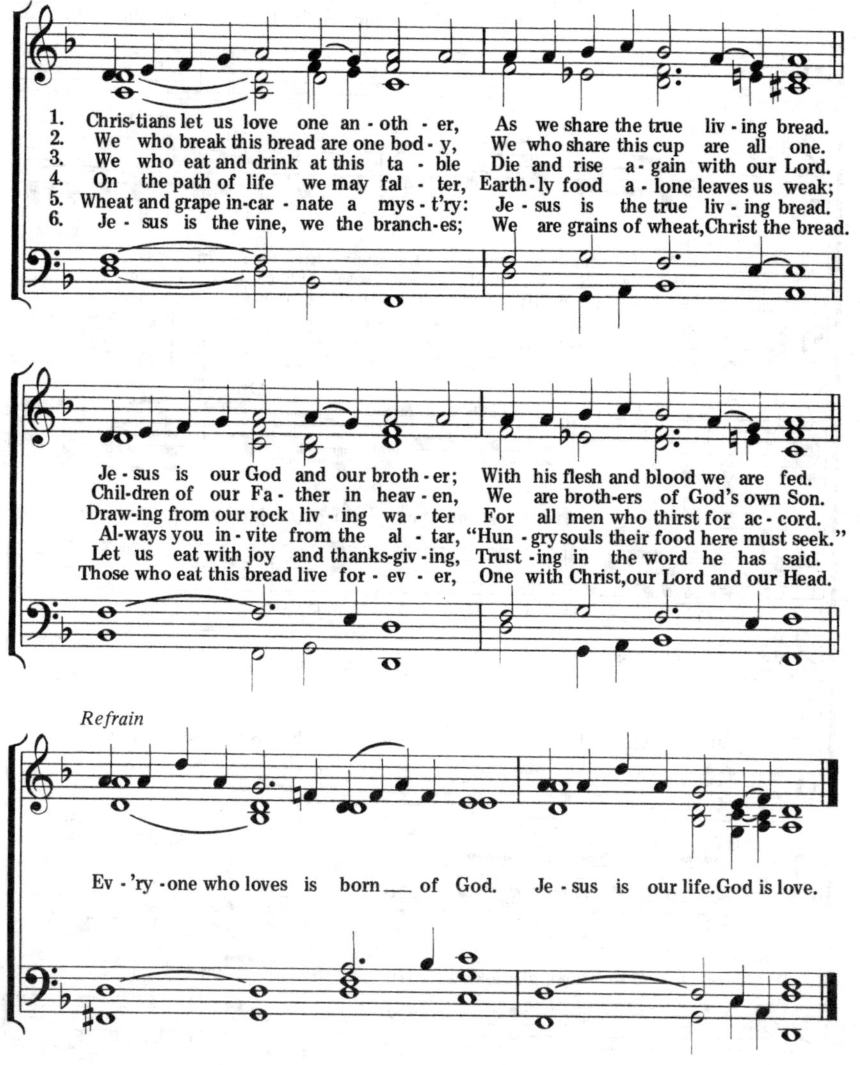
1. Chris-tians let us love one an - oth - er, As we share the true liv - ing bread.
2. We who break this bread are one bod - y, We who share this cup are all one.
3. We who eat and drink at this ta - ble Die and rise a - gain with our Lord.
4. On the path of life we may fal - ter, Earth - ly food a - lone leaves us weak;
5. Wheat and grape in-car - nate a mys - t'ry: Je - sus is the true liv - ing bread.
6. Je - sus is the vine, we the branch-es; We are grains of wheat, Christ the bread.
Je - sus is our God and our broth - er; With his flesh and blood we are fed.
Chil-dren of our Fa - ther in heav - en, We are broth-ers of God's own Son.
Draw-ing from our rock liv - ing wa - ter For all men who thirst for ac - cord.
Al-ways you in - vite from the al - tar, "Hun - gry souls their food here must seek."
Let us eat with joy and thanks-giv - ing, Trust - ing in the word he has said.
Those who eat this bread live for - ev - er, One with Christ, our Lord and our Head.
Refrain
Ev - 'ry - one who loves is born ___ of God. Je - sus is our life. God is love.

82 Communion Song

Sonny Salsbury

D
G/D
Dmaj7
1. In the up - per room, twelve men are sit - ting round the Lord.
2. For two thou - sand years be - liev - ers have re - mem-bered still
3. Ev - ery man through all of time is dead or dy - ing now;
Asus A
D
G/D
Asus
As He stands to share the meal they hear Him say,
that a Sav - ior died and rose and calls to - day.
what this good gift means: that we can live a - gain.
A
D
Dmaj7
This is my bod - y which is bro - ken for you, and for
G/D
D G
F♯m7♭5
you I've known the pain.
This wine you drink re - calls my
B7
Em
Asus A
blood that is shed, please don't let it be in vain.

Sons of God

James Thiem

Refrain

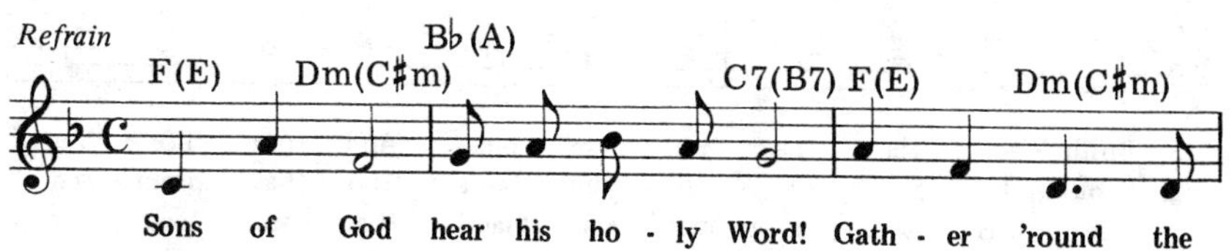
F(E) Dm(C♯m) B♭(A) C7(B7) F(E) Dm(C♯m)
Sons of God hear his ho - ly Word! Gath - er 'round the

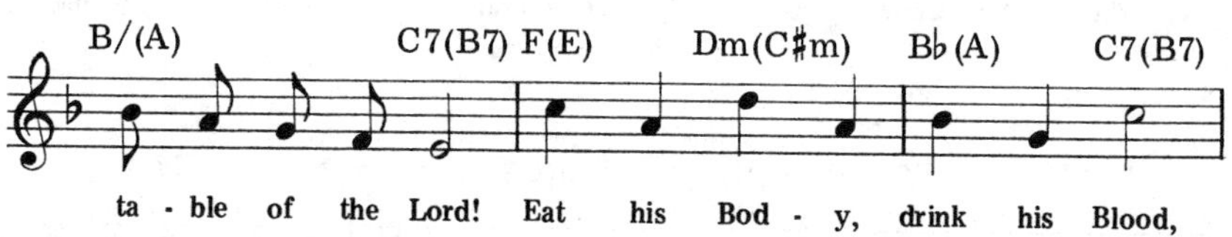
B/(A) C7(B7) F(E) Dm(C♯m) B♭(A) C7(B7)
ta - ble of the Lord! Eat his Bod - y, drink his Blood,

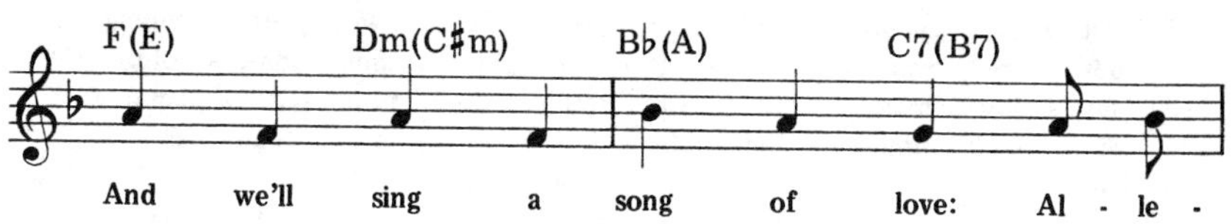
F(E) Dm(C♯m) B♭(A) C7(B7)
And we'll sing a song of love: Al - le -

F(E) Dm(C♯m) B♭(A) C7(B7)
lu, al - le - lu, al - le - lu, al - le - lu -

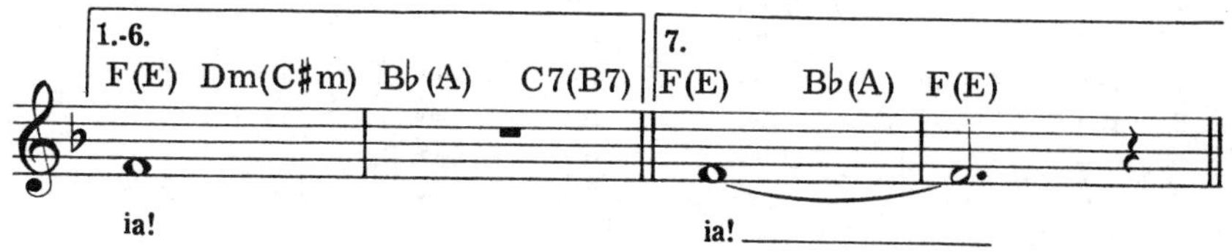
1.-6.
F(E) Dm(C♯m) B♭(A) C7(B7)
ia!
7.
F(E) B♭(A) F(E)
ia!

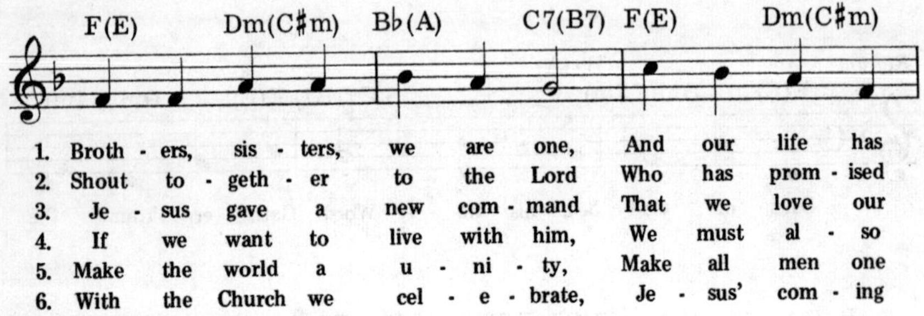
F(E) Dm(C♯m) B♭(A) C7(B7) F(E) Dm(C♯m)
1. Broth - ers, sis - ters, we are one, And our life has
2. Shout to - geth - er to the Lord Who has prom - ised
3. Je - sus gave a new com - mand That we love our
4. If we want to live with him, We must al - so
5. Make the world a u - ni - ty, Make all men one
6. With the Church we cel - e - brate, Je - sus' com - ing

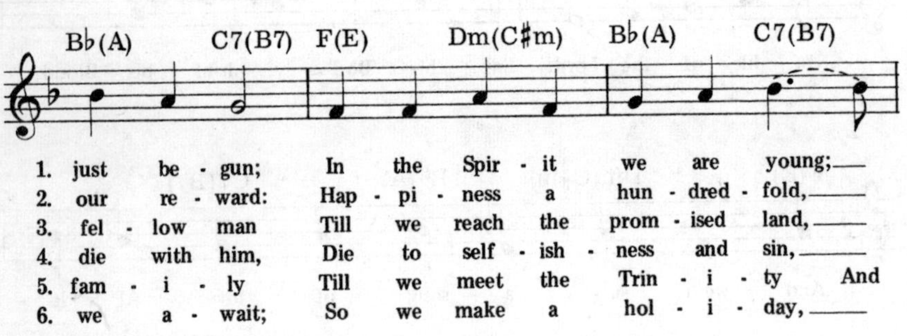
B♭(A) C7(B7) F(E) Dm(C♯m) B♭(A) C7(B7)
1. just be - gun; In the Spir - it we are young;
2. our re - ward: Hap - pi - ness a hun - dred - fold,
3. fel - low man Till we reach the prom - ised land,
4. die with him, Die to self - ish - ness and sin,
5. fam - i - ly Till we meet the Trin - i - ty And
6. we a - wait; So we make a hol - i - day,

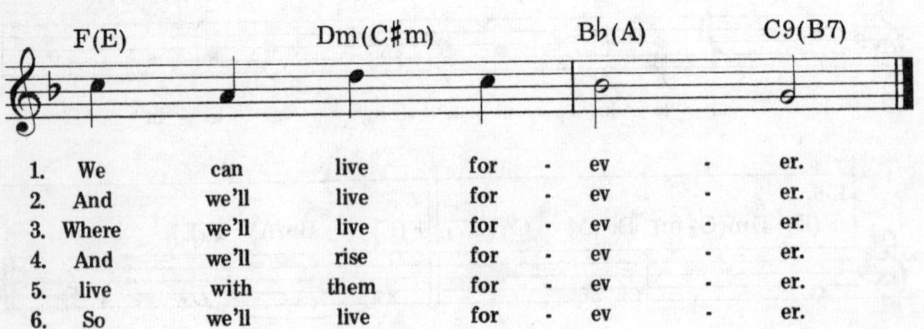
F(E) Dm(C♯m) B♭(A) C9(B7)
1. We can live for - ev - er.
2. And we'll live for - ev - er.
3. Where we'll live for - ev - er.
4. And we'll rise for - ev - er.
5. live with them for - ev - er.
6. So we'll live for - ev - er.

84 *How Lovely Is Your Dwelling Place*

Psalm 84

S. Cecil Steffen

1. How love - ly is your dwell-ing place, O Lord of hosts, My
2. And ev - en the spar-row finds a house, and the swallow a
3. How hap - py those who dwell in your house, Con -
4. O Lord of hosts will you hear my prayer, For
5. I'd rath - er be in your courts just one day, O God, than
6. For sun and shield is the Lord, our God and
1. soul yearns and pines for your courts. My heart and my flesh give a
2. nest where she puts her young. Your al - tars, O
3. tin - ual - ly they praise you. How hap - py the men whose
4. you are my hope and my shield. Now look on the face of your a -
5. spend a thou-sand a - ny-where else. I'd rath - er stand out -
6. grace and glory he be - stows. The Lord gives good things to
1. shout of joy, for the liv - ing God.
2. Lord of hosts, my King and my God.
3. strength you are their hearts are set on pilgrim - age.
4. noin - ted one, Hear my plea, O God.
5. side your door than live in the tents of sin - ners.
6. those who are sin-cere, Hap - py the man who trusts you.

When this psalm is used at Communion, the first verse may be sung as a refrain.

85 *I Am the Bread of Life*

John 6

S. Suzanne Toolan

1. I am the Bread of life. He who
2. The bread that I will give is my
3. Un - less you eat of the
4. For my flesh is food in - deed, and my
5. As the liv - ing Fa - ther sent me, and as I
6. I am the Res - ur - rec - tion
7. Yes, Lord, I be - lieve that
8. I am the way and the truth
1. comes to me shall not hun - ger; he who be -
2. flesh for the life of the world, and he who
3. flesh of the Son of Man and
4. blood is drink in - deed. He who
5. live be - cause of the Fa - ther, so
6. I am the life. He who be -
7. you are the Christ, the
8. I am the life.

1. lieves in me shall not thirst. No - one can come to
2. eats of this bread, he shall live for -
3. drink of his blood, and drink of his
4. eats of my flesh and drinks of my
5. he who eats me shall live be - cause of
6. lieves in me, ev - en if he
7. Son of God, Who have
8. No - one comes to the Fa-ther ex - cept he comes through

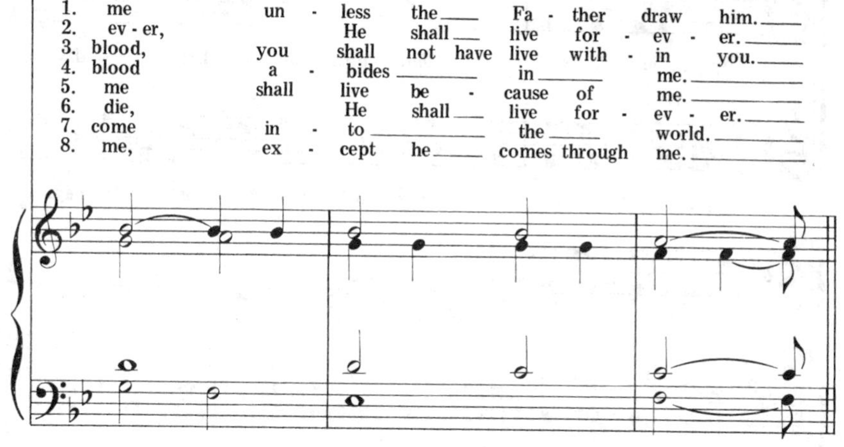
1. me un - less the Fa - ther draw him.
2. ev - er, He shall live for - ev - er.
3. blood, you shall not have live with - in you.
4. blood a - bides in me.
5. me shall live be - cause of me.
6. die, He shall live for - ev - er.
7. come in - to the world.
8. me, ex - cept he comes through me.

And I will raise him up, and I will raise him
And I will raise him up, and I will raise him
up, and I will raise him up on the last day.
up, and I will raise him up on the last day.

Take and Eat

Moderate pace

Words and music: Stephen Robinson

C Em F G7 C Em F G7 C Em F G7
Chorus: Take and eat this is my bo-dy,
C Em F G7 C Em F G7
Take and drink, this is my blood. When ev-er you do this,
C G7 C (Last Time) C G7 C
Please re-mem-ber Me. Me.
C Em F G7 C Em
1. On that Ho-ly Night be-fore you died, You gave your self to
F G7 C Em F G7
us, A gift of love. Chorus
C Em F G7 C Em
2. Now all as one we cel-e-brate, The Ho-ly Sac-ri-
F G7 C Em F G7
-fice, You gave to us. Chorus
C Em F G7 C Em
3. Christ you are our ho-ly food, The ve-ry life of
F G7 C Em F G7
man, The bread of life. Chorus
C Em F G7 C Em
4. Glo-ry to the Fa-ther and the Son, And to the Ho-ly
F G7 C Em F G7
Spir-it, God three in one. Chorus

87 *God and Man at Table Are Sat Down*

Bob Stamps

1. O wel-come all ye no-ble saints of old,
As now be-fore your ver-y eyes un-fold,
The won-ders all so long a-go fore-told.

1.
2.
D.C.
2, 3, 4, 5, 6 God and man at ta - ble are sat down.
down.

2. Elders, martyrs, all are falling down;
Prophets, patriarchs are gathering 'round,
What angels longed to see now man has found.
:: God and man at table are sat down::

3. Who is this who spreads the victory feast?
Who is this who makes our warring cease?
Jesus, Risen Savior, Prince of Peace!
::God and man at table are sat down::

4. Beggars, lame, and harlots also here;
Repentant publicans are drawing near:
Wayward sons come home without a fear.
:: God and man at table are sat down::

5. Worship in the presence of the Lord
With joyful songs and hearts in one accord.
And let our Host at table be adored.
:: God and man at table are sat down::

6. When at last this earth shall pass away,
When Jesus and His bride are one to stay,
The feast of love is just begun that day.
:: God and man at table are sat down::

88 *A Mighty Fortress Is Our God*

Martin Luther

1. A might - y for - tress is — our God, A bul-wark nev - er — fail - ing;
2. Did we in our own strength confide, Our striving would be — los - ing;
Our help - er He, — a - mid — the flood Of mor - tal ills pre - vail - ing.
Were not the right — Man on — our side, The man of God's own — choos - ing.
For still our an - cient foe Doth seek to work us woe; His craft and pow'r are great,
Dost ask who that may be? Christ Je - sus, it is He; Lord Sabaoth is His name,
And, armed with cru - el hate, On earth is not his — e - qual.
From age to age — the same, And He must win the — bat - tle.

89 *All Things Through Christ*

H.W.G.

Homer W. Grimes

I can do all things thru Christ who strength-en-eth me;
I can do all things thru Christ who strength-en - eth me.
Day by day, hour by hour, I am kept in His pow'r;
I can do all things thru Christ who strength-en-eth me.

90 *Amazing Grace!*

John Newton

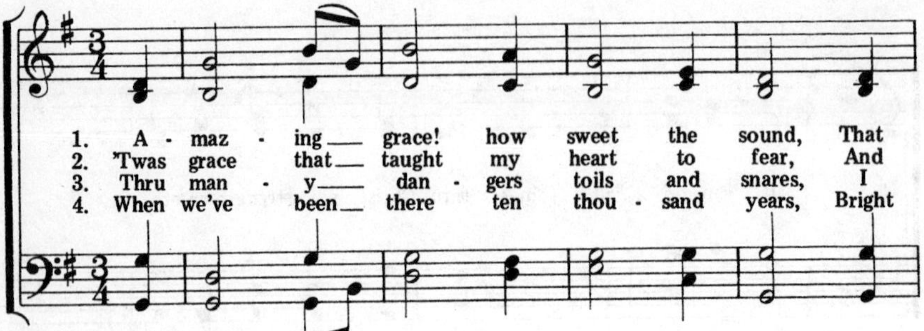

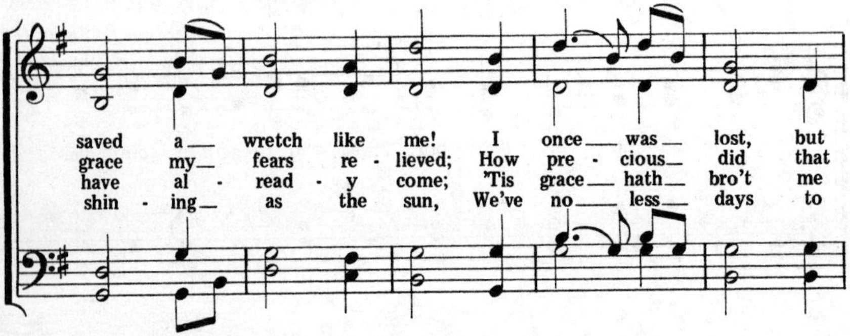

1. A - maz - ing grace! how sweet the sound, That saved a wretch like me! I once was lost, but now am found, Was blind, but now I see.
2. 'Twas grace that taught my heart to fear, And grace my fears re - lieved; How pre - cious did that grace ap - pear The hour I first be - lieved!
3. Thru man - y dan - gers toils and snares, I have al - read - y come; 'Tis grace hath bro't me safe thus far, And grace will lead me home.
4. When we've been there ten thou - sand years, Bright shin - ing as the sun, We've no less days to sing God's praise Than when we first be - gun.

91 *Amen (Spiritual)*

Verses

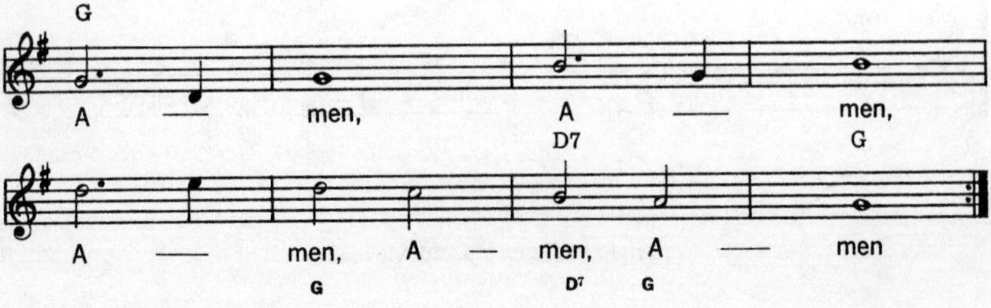

G

A — men, A — men,

D7 G

A — men, A — men, A — men

G D7 G

1. See the baby, lying in a manger on Christmas morning.
2. See Him in the temple talking to the elders. How they marveled at His wisdom!
3. See Him at the seaside, preaching and healing, to the blind and the feeble.
4. See Him in the garden praying to His Father, in deepest sorrow.
5. Yes, He is my Savior. Jesus died to save us, and He rose on Easter.

92 *Lord, Dismiss Us*

John Fawcett

J.J. Rousseau

1. Lord dis - miss us with Thy bless - ing; Fill our— hearts with
2. Thanks we— give, and a - dor - a - tion, For Thy— gos - pel's
3. So when - e'er the sig - nal's giv - en Us from— earth to
joy— and— peace; Let us— each, Thy love pos - sess - ing,
joy - ful— sound; May the— fruits of Thy sal - va - tion
call— a - way Borne on— An - gels wings to heav - en,
Tri - umph— in re - deem - ing grace: O re - fresh us,
In our— hearts and lives a bound: Ev - er— faith - ful,
Glad the— sum-mons to o - bey, May we— ev - er,
O re - fresh— us, Trav' - ling— thru this wil - der - ness.
Ev - er faith - ful, To the— truth may we— be— found.
May we ev - er Reign with— Christ in end - less— day.

93 *Blessed Is He*

Capo = 3
Barbara Richmond
Accomp. Jack Arden
Intro.
Intro.
Am
E
1. Fill all the val - leys with sun - shine, Fill all the
2. Fill all your days with thanks - giv - ing, Fill all your
3. Fill all your heart with re - joic - ing, Make room for my
Am
Dm
riv - ers with rain,
nights with your praise.
peace to take hold.
Lev - el the moun - tains
Sing to the Lord and be
Love till the pow - er of
Am
Dm
E
be - fore him, for the Lord is cre - a - ting a - gain. And
wait - ing To see him work in new ways. And
lov - ing Re- news what is emp - ty and old. And

A
D
bless - ed is he who be - lieves in the prom - ise the
E
A
E7
Lord has made un - to him. His
A
D
faith shall not go un - re - ward - ed And his
A
E7
A
love shall not be in vain.

94 *Bring Back the Springtime*

Kurt Kaiser

F
Fmaj7
Gm/F
1. When in the spring the flow'rs are bloom-ing bright and fair
2. Lord, make me like that stream that flows so cool and clear
C7
Gm/C
C7(-9)
F
Af - ter the gray of win-ter's gone,
Down from the moun-tains high a - bove,
B♭
F/A
Gm7
C7
Am
Dm
F/A
Once a-gain the lark be-gins its tun - ing
I will tell the world the won-drous sto - ry
Cm/B♭
F/A
Gm7
C7
F
E♭/F
Back in the mea-dows of my home.
Of the pre-cious stream filled with your love.

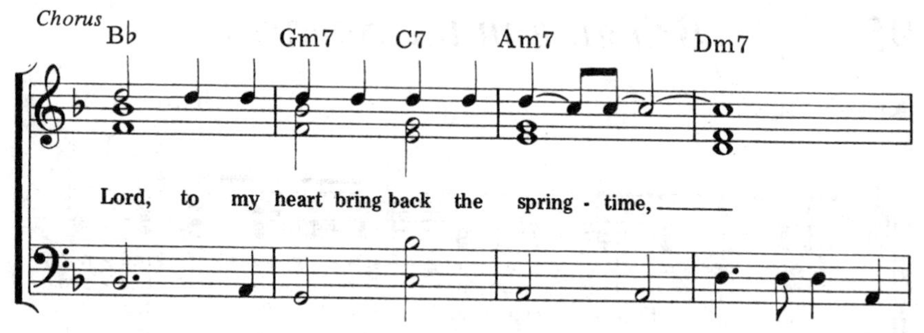
Chorus
B♭ Gm7 C7 Am7 Dm7
Lord, to my heart bring back the spring - time,

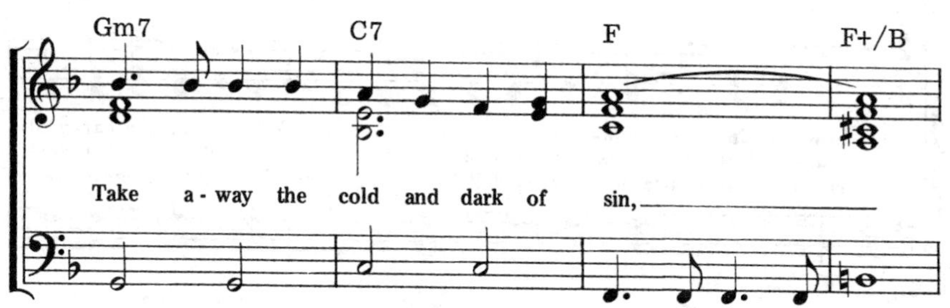
Gm7 C7 F F+/B
Take a - way the cold and dark of sin,

Gm/B♭ D7/A Gm C7 F/A A7 Dm
Oh, re - fill me now, sweet Ho - ly Spir - it,

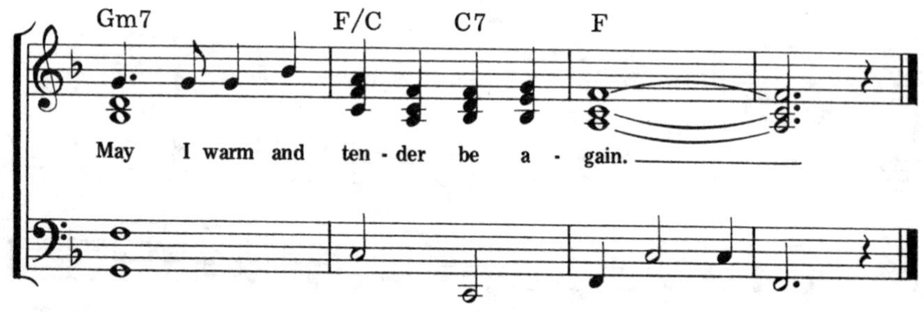
Gm7 F/C C7 F
May I warm and ten - der be a - gain.

95 *Bringing in the Sheaves*

Knowles Shaw | George A. Minor

mp
1. Sow - ing in the morn - ing, sow - ing seeds of kind - ness,
2. Sow - ing in the sun - shine, sow - ing in the shad - ows,
3. Go - ing forth with weep - ing, sow - ing for the Mas - ter,
Sow-ing in the noon-tide and the dew- y eve; Wait-ing for the har-vest,
Fear-ing neith-er clouds nor win-ter's chill-ing breeze; By and by the har-vest,
Tho' the loss sus-tained our spir-it oft - en grieves; When our weeping's o - ver,
and the time of reap-ing, We shall come re-joic-ing, Bring-ing in the sheaves.
and the la - bor end-ed, We shall come re-joic-ing, Bring-ing in the sheaves.
He will bid us wel-come, We shall come re-joic-ing, Bring-ing in the sheaves.
Chorus
Bring - ing in the sheaves, Bring - ing in the sheaves,
We shall come re-joic-ing, Bring-ing in the sheaves; Bring-ing in the sheaves,
Bring-ing in the sheaves. We shall come re-joic - ing, Bring-ing in the sheaves.

Come as a Child

David Yantis

C Am F G7
Come as a child when He calls you to fol - low, just
C Am F G7
Come as a child, for His love is un - told.
C Am F G7
Come as a child when you seek His com - mun - ion, for
C F C 1.-4. 5.
then all His bless - ings un - fold.
Verses
Em F Em C Em
1. Ev - 'ry day when I stop to pray, I think of
2. When I try to be wor - thy Lord, I know I
3. E - ven now as I think of how it must have
4. As I grow in my love for Him, it helps me
F Em C Em F
what He said, that lest you come as a
can't be - gin, un - less I seek with a
cheered Him so, to take a child in those
when I find, that as His child I am
Em A7 D7 G7
lit - tle child, His King - dom can't be had.
child - like faith, your king - dom from with - in.
strong, lov-ing arms. That love I want to know.
one with Him, and with Him joy is mine.

97 *Fill My Cup, Lord*

Richard Blanchard

Richard Blanchard
Arr. by Eugene Clark

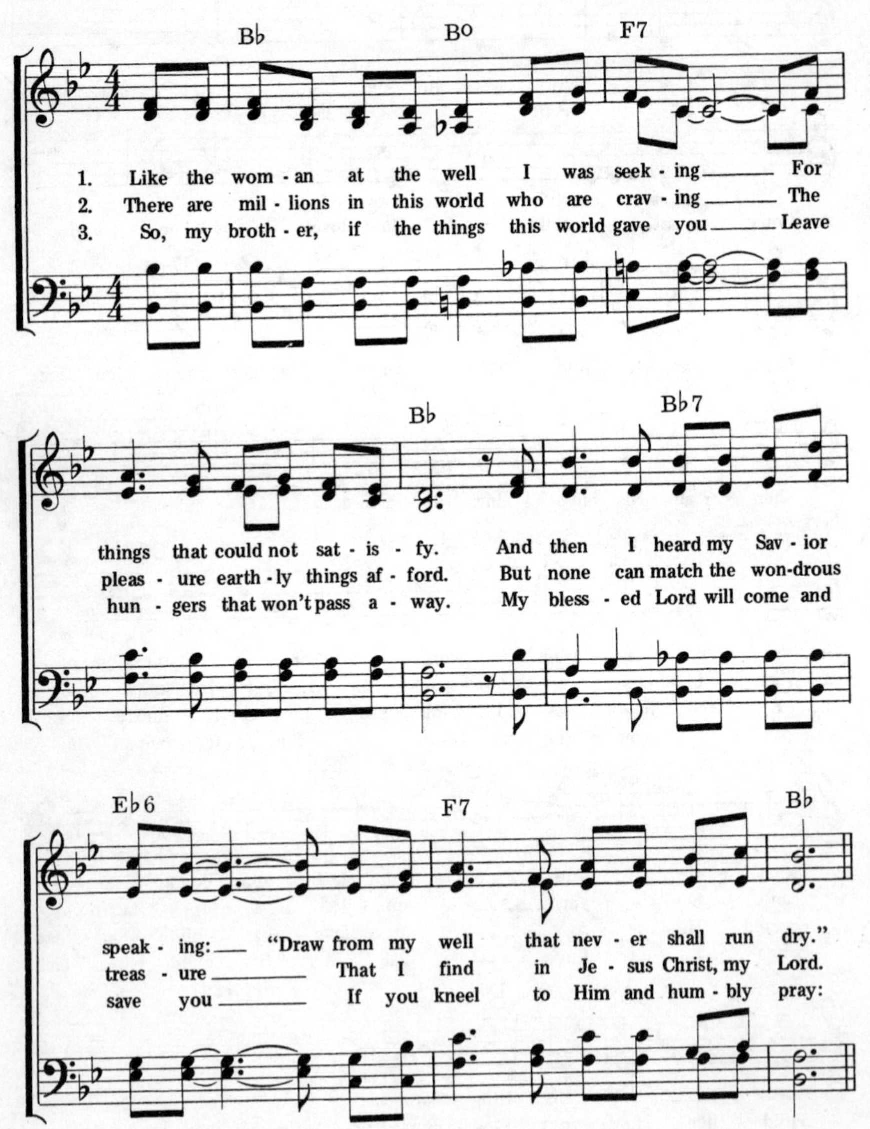

B♭ B° F7
1. Like the wom - an at the well I was seek - ing For
2. There are mil - lions in this world who are crav - ing The
3. So, my broth - er, if the things this world gave you Leave
B♭ B♭7
things that could not sat - is - fy. And then I heard my Sav - ior
pleas - ure earth - ly things af - ford. But none can match the won-drous
hun - gers that won't pass a - way. My bless - ed Lord will come and
E♭6 F7 B♭
speak - ing: "Draw from my well that nev - er shall run dry."
treas - ure That I find in Je - sus Christ, my Lord.
save you If you kneel to Him and hum - bly pray:

Chorus

F9
B♭
F7
Fill my cup, Lord, I lift it up, Lord. Come and

Cm
F7
B♭
F7
B♭
B♭7
quench this thirst-ing of my soul. Bread of heav-en, feed me till I

E♭
B♭/D
Cm7
F7
B♭
ten.
want no more. Fill my cup, fill it up and make me whole.
ten.

98 Follow Me

M.B. Sleight

Horatio R. Palmer

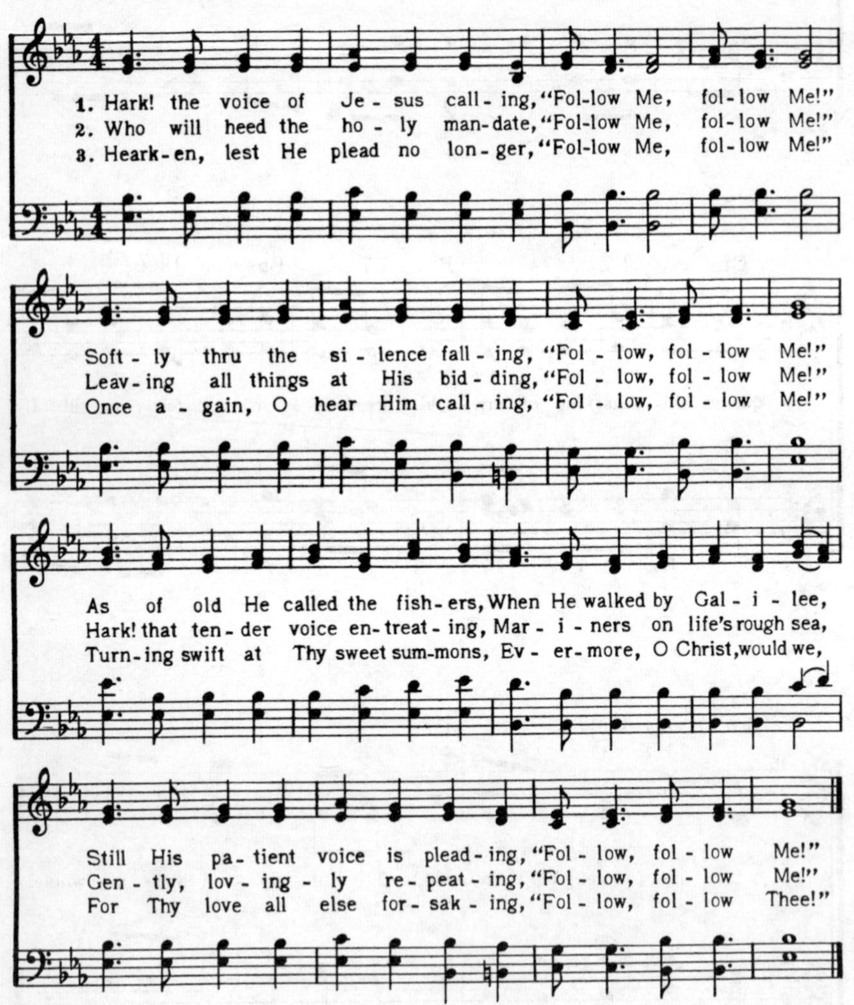
1. Hark! the voice of Je - sus call - ing, "Fol-low Me, fol - low Me!"
2. Who will heed the ho - ly man - date, "Fol-low Me, fol - low Me!"
3. Heark - en, lest He plead no lon - ger, "Fol-low Me, fol - low Me!"
Soft - ly thru the si - lence fall - ing, "Fol - low, fol - low Me!"
Leav - ing all things at His bid - ding, "Fol - low, fol - low Me!"
Once a - gain, O hear Him call - ing, "Fol - low, fol - low Me!"
As of old He called the fish - ers, When He walked by Gal - i - lee,
Hark! that ten - der voice en - treat - ing, Mar - i - ners on life's rough sea,
Turn - ing swift at Thy sweet sum-mons, Ev - er - more, O Christ, would we,
Still His pa - tient voice is plead - ing, "Fol - low, fol - low Me!"
Gen - tly, lov - ing - ly re - peat - ing, "Fol - low, fol - low Me!"
For Thy love all else for - sak - ing, "Fol - low, fol - low Thee!"

99 *For All the Blessings*

Albert H. Hutchinson | Robert N. Quaile

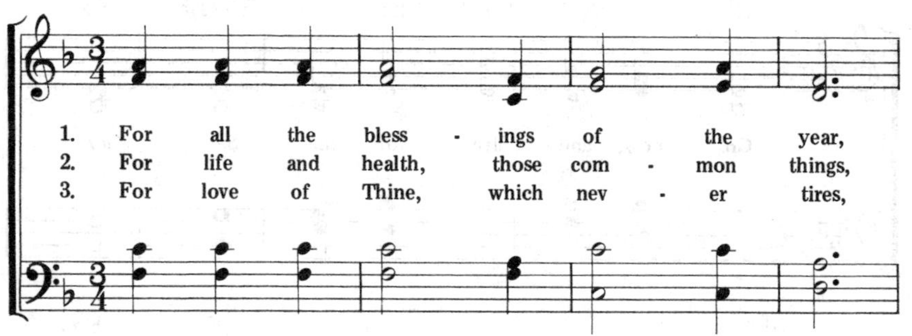
1. For all the bless - ings of the year,
2. For life and health, those com - mon things,
3. For love of Thine, which nev - er tires,

For all the friends we hold so dear, For peace on
Which ev - ery day and hour brings, For home, where
Which all our bet - ter thought in - spires, And warms our

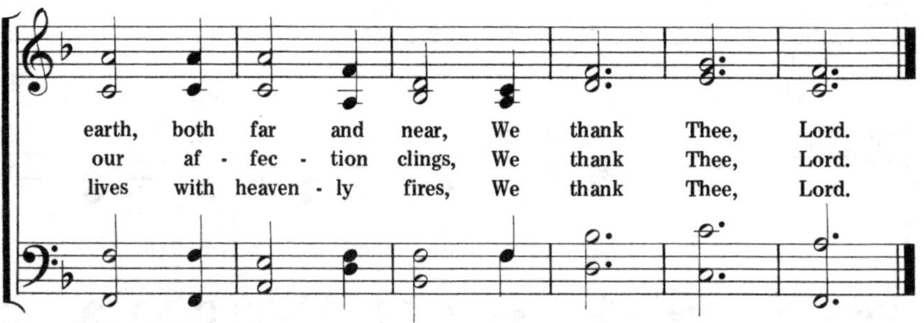
earth, both far and near, We thank Thee, Lord.
our af - fec - tion clings, We thank Thee, Lord.
lives with heaven - ly fires, We thank Thee, Lord.

100 *Go Now and Live for the Savior*

Kurt Kaiser

Eb Bb7/F Eb/G Eb Eb/Bb Bb
Go now, and live for the Sav - ior;
Bb7 Eb Eb7
Go, may this joy be your joy too.
Ab Fm7 Gm7 C7
Go, may this pres-ence ev - er guide you;
Fm7 Bb7 Eb
Go, live this life the whole day through.

101 *Grafted on the Vine (Asperges)*

C. Uehlein

1. May this wa - ter keep us a - ware
2. Wa - ter and the Spir - it give birth
3. Let us praise our Fa - ther a - bove
1. Of the gift that we all share:
2. To a life of great - er worth,
3. Who, in his ex - tra - va - gant love,
1. Graft - ed are we on Christ, the Vine,
2. For by them God's King - dom is ours
3. Sent his Spir - it and his Son;
1. By the liv - ing wa - ter's sign!
2. And we share his ho - ly pow'rs!
3. In the wa - ter, made us one!

Song for the Rite of Sprinkling with Holy Water at Sunday Mass.
May also be used for Baptismal Service.

102 *Heart Speaks to Heart*

Dedicated to Brother John Sweeney, S.S.G.

Lawrence Gross

Stephen Robinson

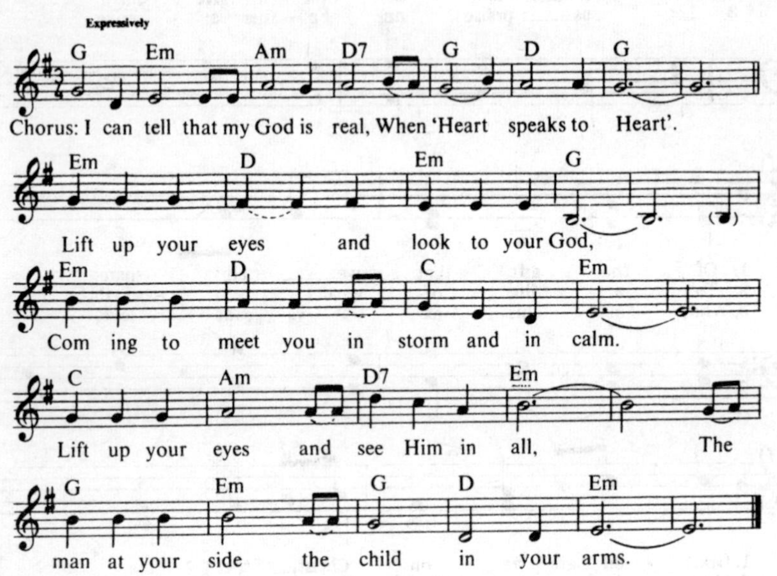
Expressively
G Em Am D7 G D G
Chorus: I can tell that my God is real, When 'Heart speaks to Heart'.
Em D Em G
Lift up your eyes and look to your God,
Em D C Em
Com ing to meet you in storm and in calm.
C Am D7 Em
Lift up your eyes and see Him in all, The
G Em G D Em
man at your side the child in your arms.

Set free your heart and open to all,
The rush of the Spirit now making all new
Be simple, be kind, a child before God,
A growing in love for man and for life.

103

Hymn for Renewal

D. Browne

Refrain: With spirit
C G C G
Op-en your eyes and see Op-en your eyes and hear
C G F C G C
Op-en your hearts, and show The love that drives out fear.
Verse:
Am E Am C
Spi-rit of light and truth Pierce through the darkness of our minds So that
F C G C D G
pray-ing to-geth-er, Search-ing to-geth-er We res-pond to the needs of our times.

2. Spirit of hope and peace
   Drive out confusion and fear
   So that working together, building together
   We bear witness that the Lord is near.

3. Spirit of joy and love
   Break through the hardness of our hearts
   So that loving together, sharing together
   We draw men to the gospel of Christ.

4. Spirit of strength and life
   Give us the courage to endure
   So that striving together, hoping together
   We unite in the service of the Lord.

104 I Saw the New Jerusalem

Rev. 21:2-4, 17, 20 Keith Clark, O.F.M.Cap., Accompaniment Jack Arden

Refrain
F
Dm
I saw the New Je - ru - sa - lem com-ing down from our
F C7 B♭ C7 F B♭ F
God, a - dorned like a bride pre-pared to meet her hus - band!
F Am F Dm Gm F C7 B♭ F
1. Ev - 'ry tear shall be wiped from your eyes, and there will be no more sor-row!
F Am C F Dm F C7 B♭ F
2. I give the wa - ter of life to an - y one who is thirst - y.

F Am F Dm F C7 B♭ F
3. By day the gates will_nev-er be closed, and there will be no night there!
F Am F Dm F C7 B♭ F
4. Ver-y soon I will be with_ you to re-ward the de-serv-ing!
F Am C F Dm Gm F C7 B♭ F
5. I will be your God and you will be my_ peo-ple!
F Am F Dm F C7 B♭ F
6. The Spir-it and the Bride say:_"Come!" Let all who hear say:"Come, Lord Je-sus!"

105 *Joyful, Joyful, We Adore Thee*

Henry van Dyke

Ludwig van Beethoven

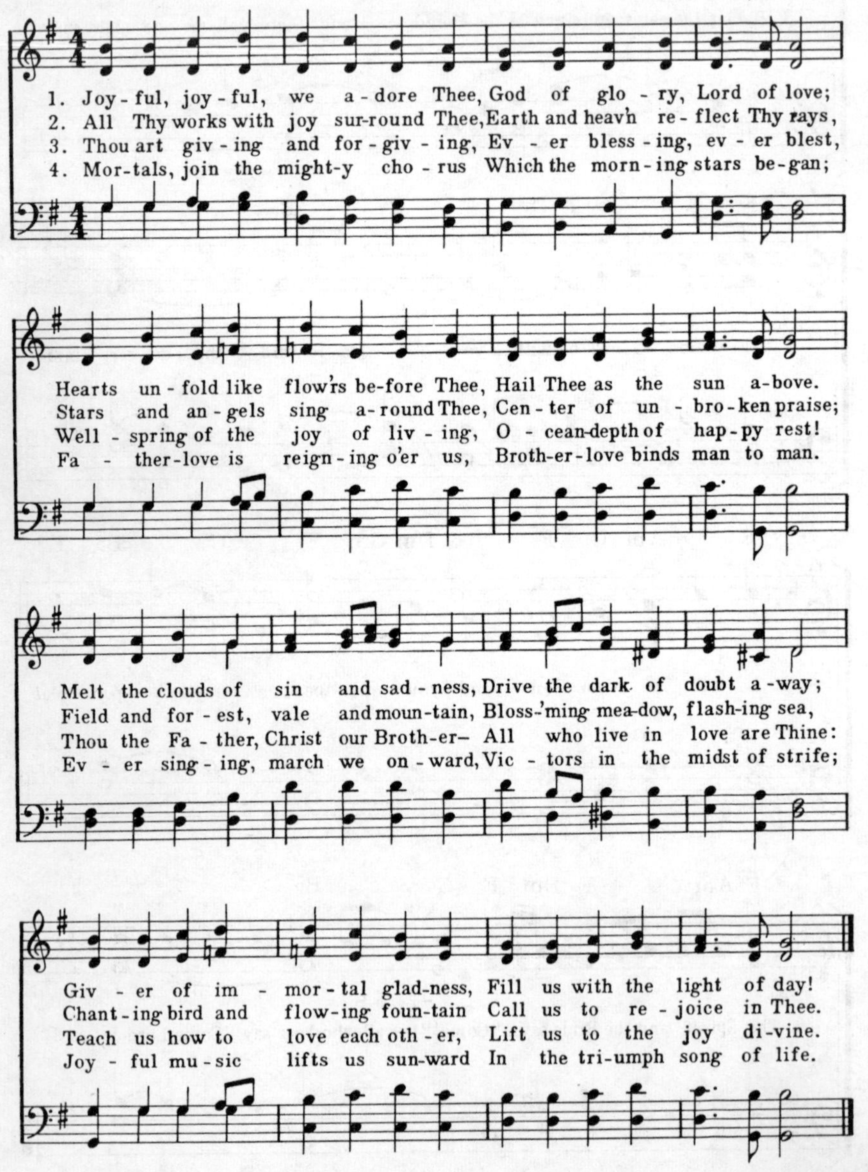
1. Joy - ful, joy - ful, we a - dore Thee, God of glo - ry, Lord of love;
2. All Thy works with joy sur-round Thee, Earth and heav'n re - flect Thy rays,
3. Thou art giv - ing and for - giv - ing, Ev - er bless - ing, ev - er blest,
4. Mor-tals, join the might-y cho - rus Which the morn - ing stars be-gan;
Hearts un - fold like flow'rs be-fore Thee, Hail Thee as the sun a-bove.
Stars and an - gels sing a-round Thee, Cen - ter of un - bro - ken praise;
Well - spring of the joy of liv - ing, O - cean-depth of hap-py rest!
Fa - ther-love is reign - ing o'er us, Broth-er-love binds man to man.
Melt the clouds of sin and sad - ness, Drive the dark of doubt a - way;
Field and for - est, vale and moun-tain, Bloss-'ming mea-dow, flash-ing sea,
Thou the Fa - ther, Christ our Broth-er– All who live in love are Thine:
Ev - er sing - ing, march we on - ward, Vic - tors in the midst of strife;
Giv - er of im - mor - tal glad-ness, Fill us with the light of day!
Chant - ing bird and flow-ing foun-tain Call us to re - joice in Thee.
Teach us how to love each oth - er, Lift us to the joy di-vine.
Joy - ful mu - sic lifts us sun-ward In the tri-umph song of life.

106 *Let All That Is Within Me Cry Holy*

Capo = 3

Anonymous, Accompaniment Jack Arden

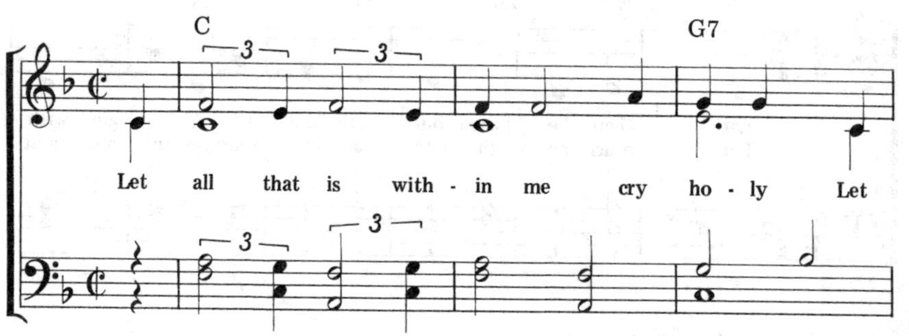
C
G7
Let all that is with - in me cry ho - ly Let

C
all that is with - in me cry ho - ly. Ho - ly,

G7
C
F
G7
C
ho - ly, ho - ly is the Lamb that was slain.

2. Let all that is within me cry worthy . . .
3. Let all that is within me cry Jesus . . .
4. Let all that is within me cry glory . . . glory, glory, glory *to* the Lamb that was slain.

107 *Let There Be Peace on Earth*

Sy Miller and Jill Jackson
Slowly
C Am Dm7 G7 C F Em C
Let there be peace on earth And let it be - gin with
Let peace be - gin with me, Let this be the mo - ment
Dm G7 C B7 Em
me; Let there be peace on earth, The peace that was
now. With ev - 'ry step I take, Let this be my
B7 G7 1. Am Em
meant to be. With God as our Fa - ther,
sol - emn vow: To
C7 F G7 C Am7
Broth - ers all are we. Let me

D7 G Am D7 G7
walk with my broth-er In per-fect har-mo-ny.
2. C C7 F
take each mo-ment and live each mo-ment in peace e-
Fdim Am D Fm C E F
ter-nal-ly. Let there be peace on
C C7 F E Am Dm C
earth and let it be-gin with me.

108 *Like a Lamb Who Needs the Shepherd*

Ralph Carmichael

C
Dm7
C
1. Where He leads me I must fol - low
2. Life is like a wind - ing path - way
3. Tho you walk through dark - est val - leys
C
Dm7
C
With - out Him I'd lose my way.
Who can tell what lies a - head
And the sky is cold and gray
F
C
I will see a bright to - mor - row
Will it lead to shad - y pas - tures
Tho you climb the steep - est moun - tains
Dm
A7
Dm7
G7
C
If I fol - low Him to - day.
or to wil - der - ness in - stead
He will nev - er let you stray

Am Em F C
Like A Lamb Who Needs The Shep - herd
Like A Lamb Who Needs The Shep - herd
Like A Lamb Who Needs The Shep - herd
Am6 B+ B7 Em F D7 G7
At His side I'll al - ways stay
When in - to the night I go
By your side He'll al - ways stay
C Dm7 C
Thru the night His strength I'll bor - row
Help me find the path that's nar - row
Till the end of life's long jour - ney
Am C G7 C
Then I'll see an - oth - er day.
While I trav - el here be - low.
He will lead you all the way.

109 *Onward, Christian Soldiers*

Sabine Baring-Gould — Arthur Sullivan

1. On-ward, Christian sol - diers! Marching as to war, With the cross of
2. Like a might - y ar - my Moves the Church of God; Brothers, we are
3. Crowns and thrones may perish, Kingdoms rise and wane; But the Church of
4. On-ward, then, ye peo - ple! Join our happy throng; Blend with ours your
Je - sus Go - ing on be - fore; Christ, the roy - al Mas - ter,
tread - ing Where the saints have trod; We are not di - vid - ed,
Je - sus Con-stant will re - main; Gates of hell can nev - er
voic - es In the tri-umph song; Glo - ry, laud, and hon - or,
Leads a-gainst the foe; For-ward in - to bat - tle, See, His banners go!
All one bod - y we; One in hope and doc - trine, One in char - i - ty.
'Gainst that Church prevail; We have Christ's own promise, Which can never fail.
Un - to Christ the King; This thro' countless a - ges Men and an - gels sing.
Chorus
On-ward, Chris-tian sol - diers! March-ing as to war,
With the cross of Je - sus Go - ing on be - fore.

110 *Our Father*

Br. Charles Naparalla

G A D G C
Our Fa - ther, who art in hea - ven hal - lowed
D G C D
be Thy name. Thy king - dom come, Thy
G C D C G
will be done, on earth as in heav - en.
G A D G C
Give us this day our dai - ly bread and for -
D G C D
give us our faults As we for - give those who
G C D C
harm us, and lead us not in - to temp - ta -
G C D G C G
tion But de - liv - er us from death.

Pass It On

Kurt Kaiser

D F♯m G A
1. It on - ly takes a spark to get a fire go - ing
2. won-drous time is spring when all the trees are bud - ding
3. wish for you my friend this hap - pi - ness that I've found
D F♯m G
And soon all those a - round can warm up in its
The birds be - gin to sing; The flow - ers start their
You can de - pend on Him, It mat - ters not where
A D G D/F♯
glow - ing That's how it is with God's love
bloom - ing That's how it is with God's love
you're bound I'll shout it from the moun-tain top
Em A F♯m Bm Em7
Once you've ex - per - i - enced it you spread His love to
Once you've ex - per - i - enced it you want to sing it's
I want my world to know; The Lord of love has

D/F♯ G A
1.&2.
D
ev - 'ry - one; You want to pass it on. 2. What a
fresh like spring; You want to pass it on. 3. I
come to me, I want to pass it on.
3.
D G D/F♯
I'll shout it from the moun - tain top
Em A F♯m Bm Em7 D/F♯
I want my world to know,– The Lord of love has come to me, I
G A D
want to pass it on.

112 Prayer of St. Francis

Sebastian Temple. Accomp. Jack Arden

C
1. Make me a chan-nel of your peace. Where
2. Make me a chan-nel of your peace. Where
G7
there is hat-red let me bring your love. Where
there's des-pair in life, let me bring hope. Where
there is in-ju-ry, your par-don, Lord. And
there is dark-ness on-ly light, And
1.
C F C
where there's doubt, true faith in you.
where there's sad-ness ev-er

2.
C
F
C
F
joy.
Oh, Mas - ter, grant that I may nev - er
C
G7
seek
So much to be con - soled as to con -
C
C7
F
sole.
To be un - der - stood as to un - der -
C
D7
stand
To be loved as to love, with all my

G7
C
soul.
3. Make me a chan - nel of your
peace.
It is in par - don - ing that we are
G7
par - doned. In giv - ing to all men that we re - ceive,
C
And in dy - ing that we're born to e-ter - nal life.

113 *Song for Evening*

C. Uehlein

D G D G
1. Now that the day is near - ly done, We pray to Christ, God's
2. Al - ways pro - tect us with your might; In love and truth, our
3. In eve - ry per - son, let us know you, So at life's end you'll
C D G D
on - ly Son: Where - ev - er we must spend the night,
hearts u - nite! Nev - er let night of sin in our soul;
know us too! When at long last our la - bor shall end,
D Bm C D C D
Stay with us, Lord, our hope, our light! A - men.
Light of the World, lead to our goal! A - men.
Come to us, Lord, e - ter - nal friend! A - men.

114 *Sing Out to God*

Sister Philip

Refrain:
C F C
Sing out to God, Sing .out your love to him,
F C F C
Sing out your joy in the Liv-ing God.
Verse:
Cm G7 Cm F Cm
God you are a migh-ty God, Al-le-lu-ia.
E♭ Cm Gm Cm B♭ Cm
build in us your king-dom of love, Al-le-l-u-ia.

2. God your love is a mighty love, Alleluia
   It embraced the cross, for the love of us, Alleluia.

3. God your word is a mighty word, Alleluia.
   It has recreated the face of the earth, Alleluia.

115 *Standin' in the Need of Prayer*

Spiritual

mf
It's me, O Lord, It is me, O Lord, Stand-in' in the need of pray'r; It's
mf

me, O Lord, It is me, O Lord, I'm a-stand-in' in the need of pray'r. Not my
fa-ther, not my moth-er, But it's me, O Lord, Stand-in' in the need of pray'r, Not my
sis-ter, not my broth-er, But it's me, O Lord, Stand-in' in the need of pray'r. It's
me, O Lord, It is me, O Lord, Stand-in' in the need of pray'r; It's
me, O Lord, It is me, O Lord, I'm a-stand-in' in the need of pray'r.

116 Take My Life

Francis R. Havergal

Louis J. F. Herold. Arr. George Kingsley

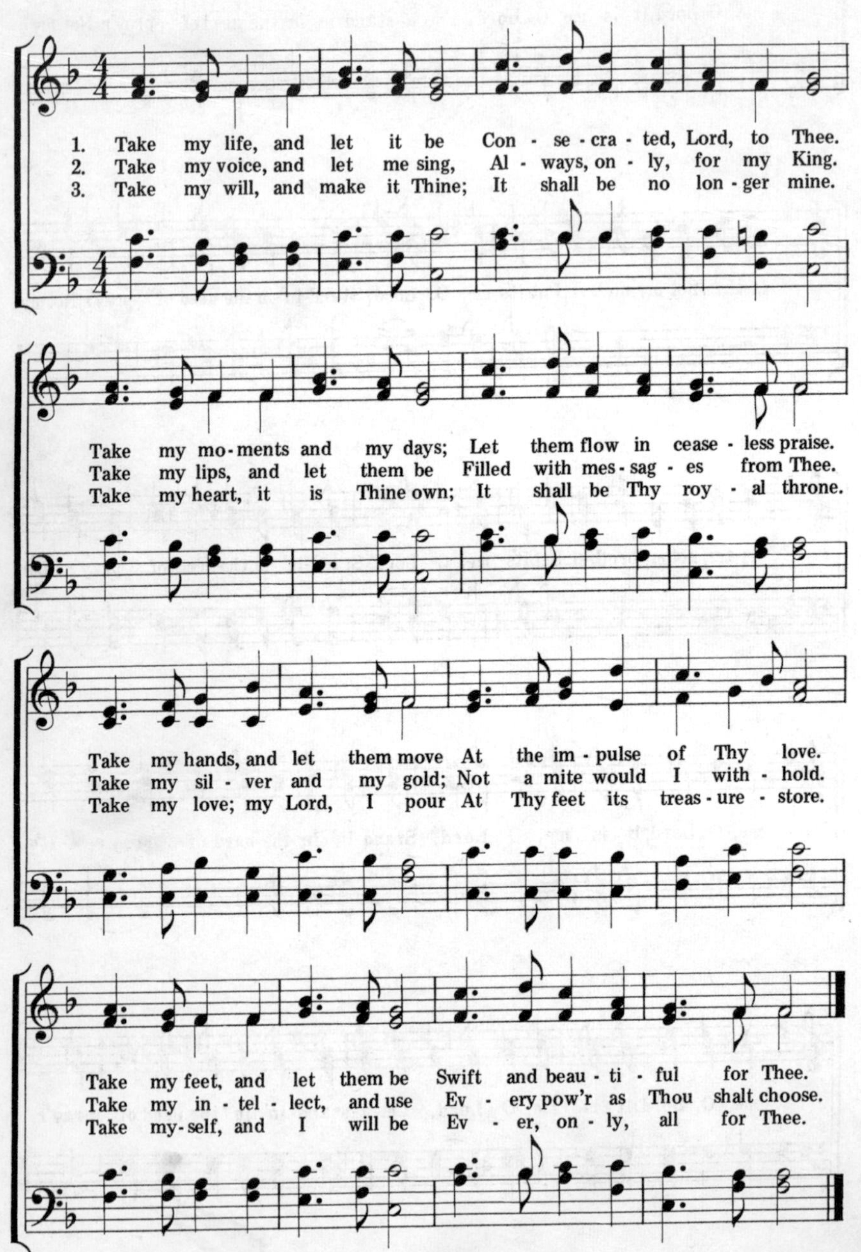
1. Take my life, and let it be Con - se - cra - ted, Lord, to Thee.
2. Take my voice, and let me sing, Al - ways, on - ly, for my King.
3. Take my will, and make it Thine; It shall be no lon - ger mine.
Take my moments and my days; Let them flow in cease - less praise.
Take my lips, and let them be Filled with mes - sag - es from Thee.
Take my heart, it is Thine own; It shall be Thy roy - al throne.
Take my hands, and let them move At the im - pulse of Thy love.
Take my sil - ver and my gold; Not a mite would I with - hold.
Take my love; my Lord, I pour At Thy feet its treas - ure - store.
Take my feet, and let them be Swift and beau - ti - ful for Thee.
Take my in - tel - lect, and use Ev - ery pow'r as Thou shalt choose.
Take my - self, and I will be Ev - er, on - ly, all for Thee.

117 *There Is a Balm in Gilead*

Traditional
There is a Balm in Gil-e-ad To make the wound-ed whole;
There is a Balm in Gil-e-ad To heal a sin-sick soul.
1. Some-times you feel dis-cour-aged, And you think your work's in vain,
2. If you can-not preach like Pe-ter, If you can-not pray like Paul,
And then the Ho-ly Spir-it Re-vives your soul a-gain.
You can tell the love of Je-sus, And say, "He died for all."
CHORUS
There is a Balm in Gil-e-ad To heal the sin-sick soul.

The Savior Is Waiting

Ralph Carmichael

The Sav - ior is wait - ing to en - ter your heart.
(If) you'll take one step t'ward the Sav - ior my friend,

Why don't you let Him come in. There's
You'll find His arms o - pen wide. Re -

noth - ing in this world to keep you a - part.
cieve Him and all of your dark - ness will end.
What is your an - swer to Him.
With - in your heart He'll a - bide.
Time af - ter
time He has wait - ed be - fore And now He is
wait - ing a - gain.
To see if you're

will - ing to o - pen the door. Oh how He
wants to come in. If in
1.
2.

119 Trust and Obey

Rev. J.H. Sammis

D.B. Towner

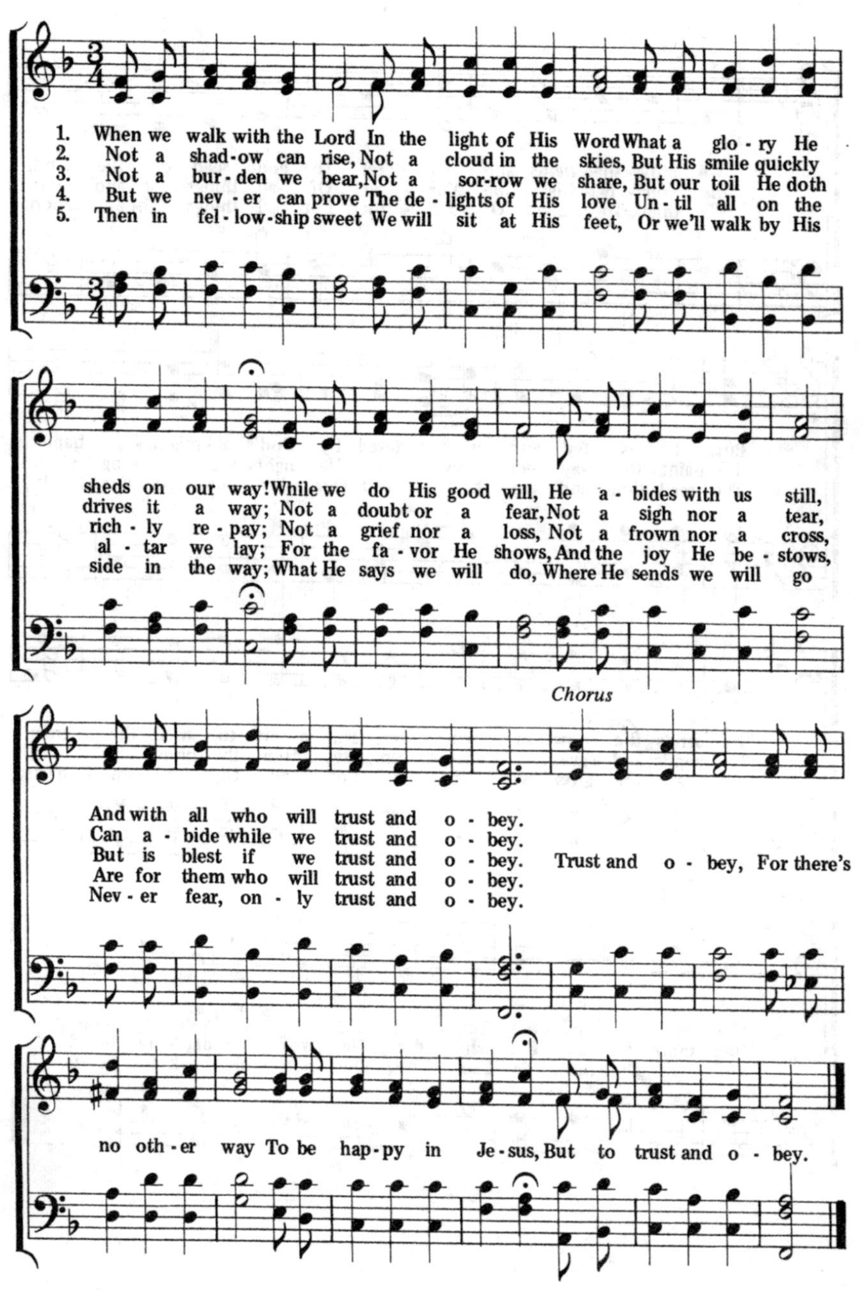

1. When we walk with the Lord In the light of His Word What a glo - ry He
2. Not a shad - ow can rise, Not a cloud in the skies, But His smile quickly
3. Not a bur - den we bear, Not a sor-row we share, But our toil He doth
4. But we nev - er can prove The de - lights of His love Un - til all on the
5. Then in fel - low - ship sweet We will sit at His feet, Or we'll walk by His
sheds on our way! While we do His good will, He a - bides with us still,
drives it a way; Not a doubt or a fear, Not a sigh nor a tear,
rich - ly re - pay; Not a grief nor a loss, Not a frown nor a cross,
al - tar we lay; For the fa - vor He shows, And the joy He be - stows,
side in the way; What He says we will do, Where He sends we will go
Chorus
And with all who will trust and o - bey.
Can a - bide while we trust and o - bey.
But is blest if we trust and o - bey.
Are for them who will trust and o - bey.
Nev - er fear, on - ly trust and o - bey.
Trust and o - bey, For there's
no oth - er way To be hap - py in Je - sus, But to trust and o - bey.

120 We Plow the Fields

Matthias Claudius. Tr. Jane M. Campbell

Johann A.P. Schulz

We plow the fields, and scat - ter The good seed on the land,
He on - ly is the Mak - er Of all things near and far;
We thank Thee, then, O Fa - ther, For all things bright and good,
But it is fed and wa - tered By God's al - might - y hand;
He paints the way - side flow - er, He lights the eve - ning star;
The seed - time and the har - vest, Our life, our health, our food;
He sends the snow in win - ter, The warmth to swell the grain,
The winds and waves o - bey Him, By Him the birds are fed;
Ac - cept the gifts we of - fer, For all Thy love im - parts,
The breez - es and the sun - shine, And soft re - fresh - ing rain.
Much more to us His chil - dren, He gives our dai - ly bread.
And, what Thou most de - sir - est, Our hum - ble, thank - ful hearts.

121 What a Friend

Joseph Scriven

Charles C. Converse

1. What a Friend we have in Je - sus, All our sins and griefs to bear!
2. Have we tri - als and temp - ta - tions? Is there trou-ble an - y - where?
3. Are we weak and heav - y - la - den, Cum-bered with a load of care?
What a priv - i - lege to car - ry Ev - 'ry-thing to God in prayer!
We should nev - er be dis - cour - aged— Take it to the Lord in prayer.
Pre-cious Sav - ior, still our ref - uge— Take it to the Lord in prayer.
O what peace we of - ten for - feit, O what need-less pain we bear,
Can we find a friend so faith - ful Who will all our sor - rows share?
Do thy friends de-spise, for-sake thee? Take it to the Lord in prayer;
All be-cause we do not car - ry Ev - 'ry-thing to God in prayer!
Je - sus knows our ev - 'ry weak-ness— Take it to the Lord in prayer.
In His arms He'll take and shield thee— Thou wilt find a sol - ace there.

122 *America, the Beautiful*

Samuel A. Ward

Katherine Lee Bates

1. O beau-ti-ful for spa - cious skies, For am-ber waves of grain, For
2. O beau-ti-ful for pil - grim feet, Whose stern, im - pas - sioned stress A
3. O beau-ti-ful for he - roes proved In lib - er - at - ing strife, Who
4. O beau-ti-ful for pa - triot dream That sees be-yond the years, Thine
pur-ple moun-tain maj - es - ties A - bove the fruit-ed plain! A -
thor-ough-fare for free-dom beat A - cross the wil-der - ness! A -
more than self their coun-try loved, And mer - cy more than life! A -
al - a - bas - ter cit - ies gleam, Un-dimmed by hu - man tears! A -
mer - i - ca! A - mer - i - ca! God shed His grace on thee, And
mer - i - ca! A - mer - i - ca! God mend thine ev - 'ry flaw, Con -
mer - i - ca! A - mer - i - ca! May God thy gold re - fine, Till
mer - i - ca! A - mer - i - ca! God shed His grace on thee, And
crown thy good with broth - er - hood From sea to shin - ing sea.
firm thy soul in self- con - trol, Thy lib - er - ty in law.
all suc-cess be no - ble - ness, And ev - 'ry gain di - vine.
crown thy good with broth - er - hood From sea to shin - ing sea.

5. Lift high the cross, unfurl the flag;
May they forever stand
United in our hearts and hopes,
God and our native land.
America! America
May God thy love increase,
Till wars are past and earth at last
May follow Christ in peace.

123 *America*

(My Country 'Tis of Thee)

Samuel F. Smith — Henry Carey

1. My coun - try, 'tis of thee, Sweet land of lib - er - ty,
2. My na - tive coun - try, thee, Land of the no - ble, free,
3. Let mu - sic swell the breeze, And ring from all the trees
4. Our fa - thers' God, to Thee, Au - thor of lib - er - ty,
Of thee I sing; Land where my fa - thers died, Land of the
Thy name I love: I love thy rocks and rills, Thy woods and
Sweet free - dom's song: Let mor - tal tongues a - wake; Let all that
To Thee we sing: Long may our land be bright With free - dom's
pil - grim's pride, From ev - ery moun - tain side Let free - dom ring!
tem - pled hills; My heart with rap - ture thrills Like that a - bove.
breathe par - take; Let rocks their si - lence break, The sound pro - long.
ho - ly light; Pro - tect us by Thy might, Great God, our King!

124 *Battle Hymn of the Republic*

Julia Ward Howe

William Steffe

Allegretto
1. Mine eyes have seen the glo - ry of the com - ing of the Lord; He is
2. In the beau - ty of the lil - ies Christ was born a-cross the sea, With a
tram-pling out the vin - tage where the grapes of wrath are stored; He hath
glo - ry in His bos - om that trans - fig - ures you and me; As He
loosed the fateful lightning of His ter - ri-ble swift sword, His truth is marching on.
died to make men holy, let us die to make men free, While God is marching on.
Glo - ry! glo - ry! Hal - le - lu - jah! Glo - ry! glo - ry! Hal - le - lu - jah!
Glo - ry! glo - ry! Hal - le - lu - jah! His truth is march-ing on.

125

Beyond a Dream

David Yantis

C F G7
1. If you looked be - yond a dream to a time when the
2. If you looked be - yond a dream to a place where the
3. If you looked be - yond a dream to a land where all
C Am F G7
world was - n't cold to hun - ger, to suf - f'ring, to
la - bor of love had laid bare the seeds of dis -
men stood with pride de - fend - ing their rights to be
C Tacet F
need, and you found be - yond a dream there were
trust, and you found be - yond a dream there were
free, and you found be - yond a dream there were
G7 C Am F
those with their hearts filled with love, who reached out to
those with their hearts seek - ing peace, had made hate a
those with their hearts born of hope, while strug - gling had
G7 C C7 F G7 C
help when they could, why, then, can't that time be now?
thing of dis - gust, why, then, can't that place be here?
found un - i - ty, why, then, can't that land be ours?
C7 F G7 C
why, then, can't that time be now?
why, then, can't that place be here?
why, then, can't that land be ours?

126 *The Star-Spangled Banner*

Francis Scott Key | John Stafford Smith

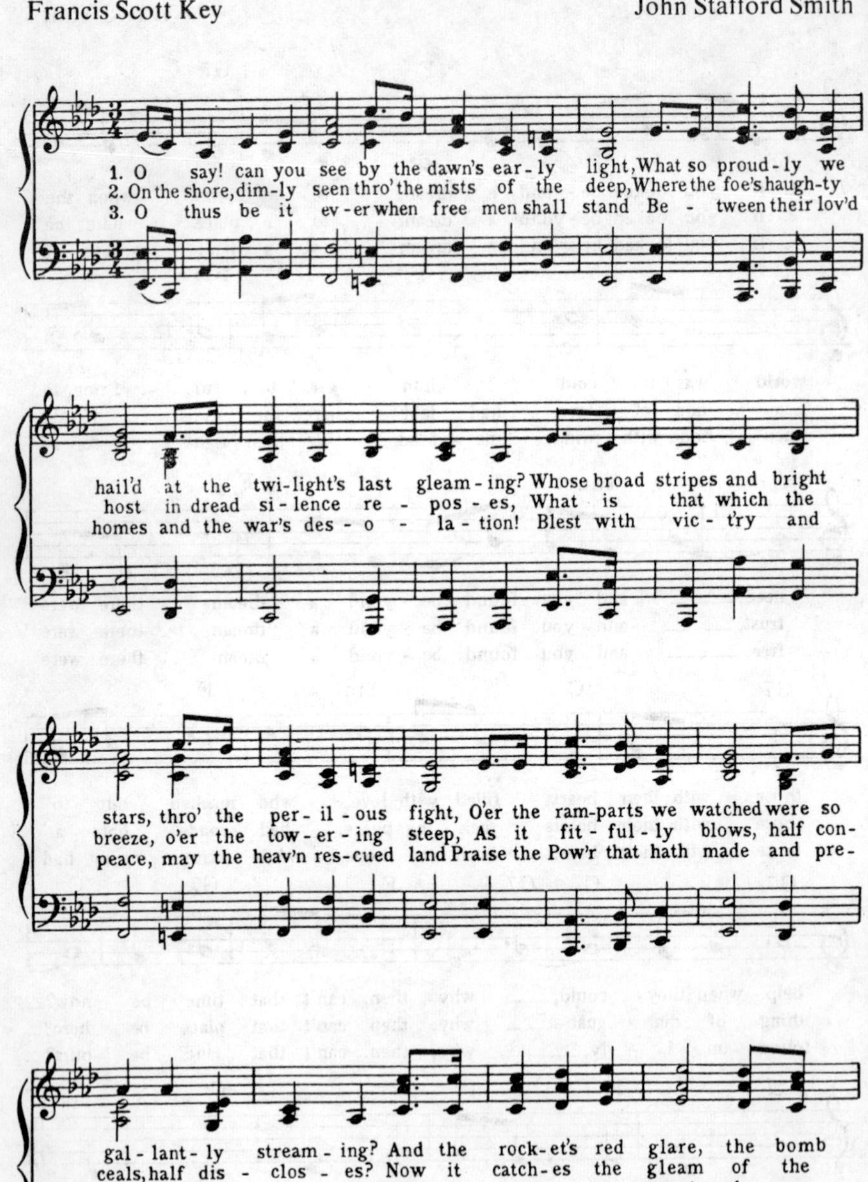
1. O say! can you see by the dawn's ear-ly light, What so proud-ly we
2. On the shore, dim-ly seen thro' the mists of the deep, Where the foe's haugh-ty
3. O thus be it ev-er when free men shall stand Be - tween their lov'd
hail'd at the twi-light's last gleam-ing? Whose broad stripes and bright
host in dread si-lence re - pos-es, What is that which the
homes and the war's des - o - la-tion! Blest with vic-t'ry and
stars, thro' the per-il-ous fight, O'er the ram-parts we watched were so
breeze, o'er the tow-er-ing steep, As it fit-ful-ly blows, half con-
peace, may the heav'n res-cued land Praise the Pow'r that hath made and pre-
gal-lant-ly stream-ing? And the rock-et's red glare, the bomb
ceals, half dis - clos - es? Now it catch-es the gleam of the
served us a na - tion! Then — con-quer we must, when our

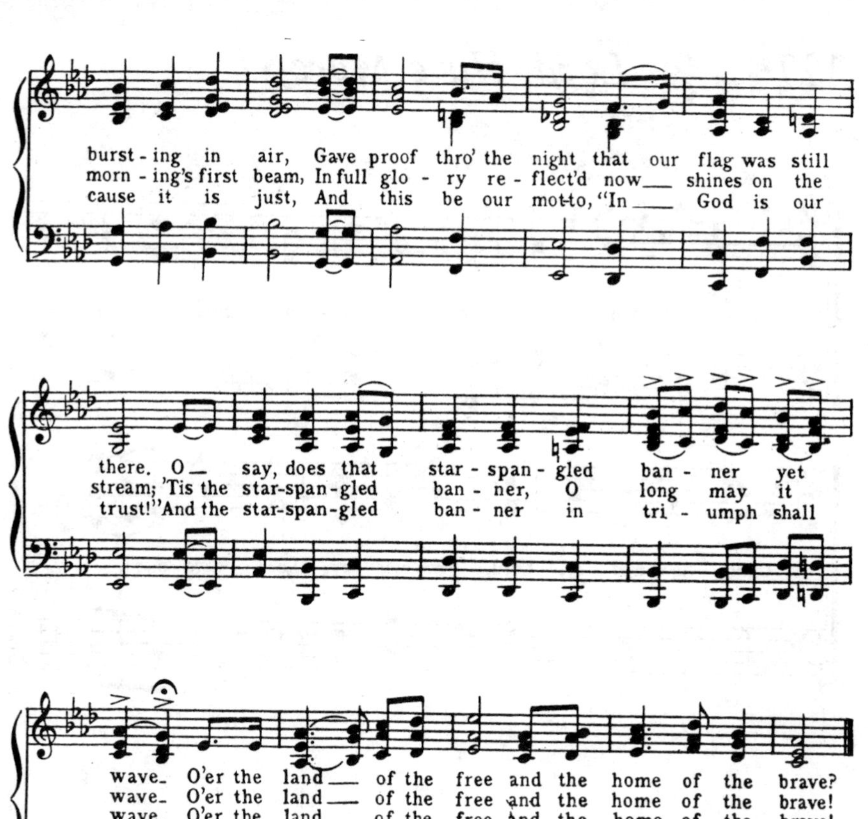
burst - ing in air, Gave proof thro' the night that our flag was still
morn - ing's first beam, In full glo - ry re - flect'd now___ shines on the
cause it is just, And this be our mot-to, "In___ God is our
there. O___ say, does that star - span - gled ban - ner yet
stream; 'Tis the star-span-gled ban - ner, O long may it
trust!" And the star-span-gled ban - ner in tri - umph shall
wave_ O'er the land___ of the free and the home of the brave?
wave_ O'er the land___ of the free and the home of the brave!
wave_ O'er the land___ of the free and the home of the brave!

127 Lord, Have Mercy 1

Lord, have mer - cy. Lord, have mer - cy. Christ, have mer - cy.
3
Christ, have mer - cy. Lord, have mer - cy. Lord, have mer - cy.
3
3

128 Lord, Have Mercy 2

Lord, have mer - cy. Christ, have mer - cy. Lord, have mer - cy.

Lord, Have Mercy 3

Lord, have mer - cy.
Christ, have mer - cy.
Lord, have mer - cy.

Note

The "Glory" (see following pages) is a very ancient hymn of Greek origin. In the East it was used in the Morning Office, not in the Eucharistic Liturgy. In the West it was at first permitted only in the Mass of Christmas. Then it found its way into Masses for Sundays and the feasts of martyrs, but only when the bishop celebrated.

Gradually this restriction was lifted and by the end of the 11th century the "Glory" was included in all Masses of festive character, whether celebrated by bishop or priest. Now once again, its special character is recognized and it is "sung on Sundays outside of Advent and Lent and on solemnities and feasts, and in celebrations of special solemnity." (General Instruction of the Roman Missal, No. 31.)

130 *Glory to God in the Highest I*

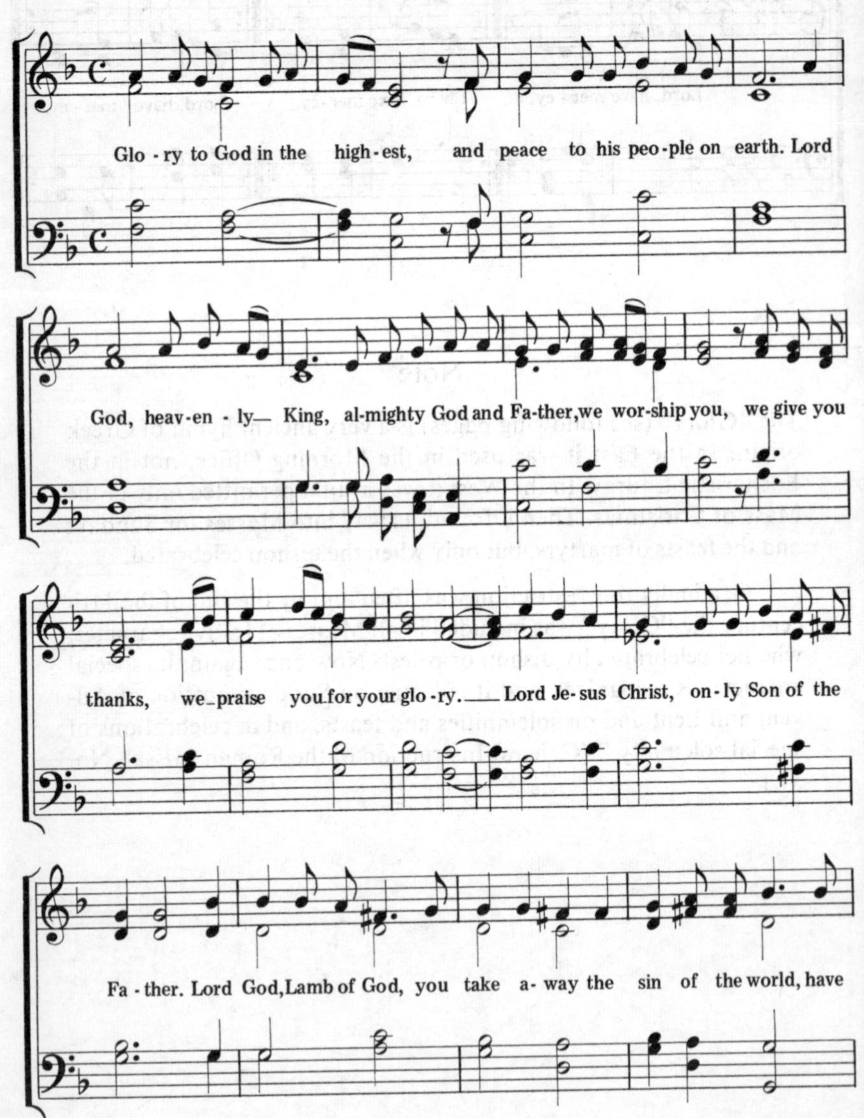
Glo - ry to God in the high - est, and peace to his peo - ple on earth. Lord
God, heav - en - ly— King, al - mighty God and Fa - ther, we wor - ship you, we give you
thanks, we_praise you_for your glo - ry. — Lord Je - sus Christ, on - ly Son of the
Fa - ther. Lord God, Lamb of God, you take a - way the sin of the world, have

mer - cy on ___ us. You are seat - ed at the right hand of the Fa - ther.
re - ceive ___ our prayer. For you a - lone ___ are the ho - ly ___ one, you a -
lone are the Lord, you a - lone ___ are the Most High, Je - sus Christ,
with the Ho - ly Spir - it in the glo - ry of God the Fa - ther. A - men.

131 *Glory to God in the Highest 2*

Glo-ry to God in the high-est, and peace to his peo-ple on
earth. Lord God, heav-en-ly King, al-might-y God and Fa-ther, we
wor-ship you, we give you thanks, we praise you for your glo-ry. Lord
Je-sus Christ, on-ly Son of the Fa-ther, Lord God, Lamb of

God, you take a-way the sin of the world: have mer-cy on us; you are
seat - ed at the right hand of the Fa - ther: re - ceive our prayer.
For you a - lone are the Ho - ly One, — you a - lone are the
Lord, you a - lone are the Most High, Je - sus Christ, with the
Ho - ly Spir - it, in the glo - ry of God the Fa - ther. A - men.

132 *Glory to God in the Highest 3*

Glo-ry to God in the high-est,___ and peace to his peo-ple on
earth. Lord God, heav-en-ly King, al-might-y God and Fa-ther,_
___ we wor-ship you:___ we give you thanks,_ we praise you for your
glo-ry___ Lord Je-sus Christ, on-ly Son of the Fa-ther,___ Lord
3
3

God, Lamb of God, you take a-way the sin of the world: have mer-cy on us: you are
seat-ed at the right hand of the Fa - ther: — re-ceive our prayer. For you a-lone are the
Ho - ly One, you a-lone are the Lord, you a - lone are the Most High, Je-sus Christ, —
— with the Ho-ly Spir-it — in the glo - ry of God the Fa - ther. — A - men.
3

Gospel Acclamations

133
Alleluia 1
Adapted by W. H. Monk, 1861
Al - le - lu - ia! Al - le - lu - ia! Al - le - lu - ia!
134
Alleluia 2
Chant
Al - le - lu - ia, Al - le - lu - ia, Al - le - lu - ia.
135
Alleluia 3
Chant
Al - le - lu - ia, Al - le - lu - ia, Al - le - lu - ia.
136
Alleluia 4
Byzantine
Al - le - lu - ia, Al - le - lu - ia, Al - le - lu - ia.

137 *Alleluia 5*

E.A.C.

Al - le - lu - - ia, Al - le lu - - ia.

During the season of Lent, instead of Alleluia, other acclamations are sung to greet Christ who comes to us in His Word.

138 *Alleluia* / 139 *Praise the Lord*

E.A.C.

Al - le - lu - ia, Al - le - lu - ia.
Praise the Lord, Oh, praise him with joy.

140a *Alleluia* / 140b *Praise to You*

E.A.C.

Al - le - lu - - ia.
Praise to you, O Lord.

141 *Praise to You, Lord Jesus Christ 1*

E.A.C.

Praise to you, Lord, Je - sus, Christ, King of end - less glo - ry.

142 *Praise to You, Lord Jesus Christ 2*

E.A.C.

Praise to you, Lord, Je - sus, Christ, King of end - less glo - ry.

143 *Praise the Lord!* 144 *The Lord Be Praised*

E.A.C.

Praise the Lord!
The Lord be praised!

Holy, Holy, Holy 1

Traditional

Ho - ly, ho - ly, ho - ly Lord, God of power and
might. Heav - en and earth are full of your glo - ry. Ho -
san - na in the high - est! Bless - ed is he who
comes in the name of the Lord. Ho - san - na in the high - est.

Holy, Holy, Holy 2

Ho - ly, ho - ly, ho - ly Lord, God of power and might.
Heav - en and earth are full of your glo - ry. Ho -
san - na in the high - est. Bless - ed is he who
comes in the name of the Lord. Ho - san - na in the high - est.

147 *Holy, Holy, Holy 3*

3
3
3
Ho - ly, ho - ly, ho - ly Lord, God of power and might.
Heav - en and earth are full of your glo - ry. Ho -
san - na in the high - est. Bless - ed is he who comes in the
name of the Lord. Ho - san - na in the high - est.

Memorial Acclamations

148 *Christ Has Died 1*

E.A.C.

1. Christ has died. Christ is ris - en. Christ will come a - gain.

149 *Christ Has Died 2*

E.A.C.

Christ has died. Christ is ris - en. Christ will come a - gain.

150 *Dying You Destroyed Our Death*

E.A.C.

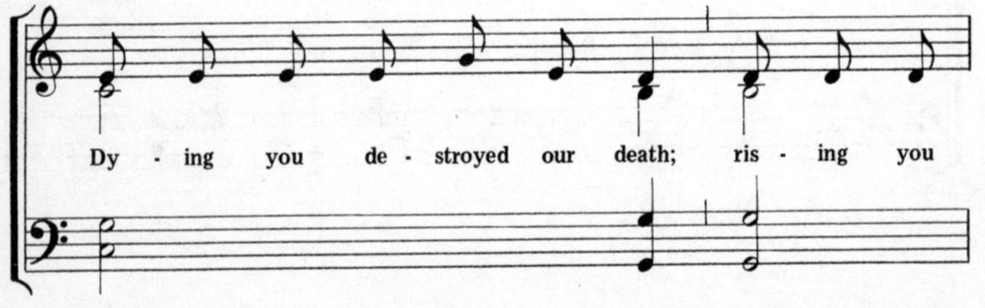
Dy - ing you de - stroyed our death; ris - ing you

re - stored our life. Lord Je - sus, come in glo - ry.

151 *When We Eat This Bread*

E.A.C.

When we eat this bread and drink this cup, we pro - claim
your death, Lord Je - sus, un - til you come in glo - ry.

152 *Lord, by Your Cross and Resurrection*

E.A.C.

Lord, by your cross and re - sur - rec - tion, you have

set us free; you are the Sav - ior of the world.

153 *We Commemorate Your Death*

Traditional

We com - mem - o - rate your death, O Lord, we ac - know-
ledge your re - sur - rec - tion and we look for your se - cond
com - ing. May your bless - ing be on us all.

Great Amens

154 Amen 1 E.A.C.
A - men, A - - men.
155 Amen 2 E.A.C.
A - - - men, A - men.
156 Danish Amen
A - men, A - men, A - - - men.
157 Dresden Amen
A - men, A - - - men.

The Lord's Prayer 1

Our Fa - ther, who art in heav-en, hal - lowed be thy name;
thy king - dom come; thy will be done on earth as it
is in heav - en. Give us this day our dai - ly bread;
and for - give us our tres - pass -es as we for-give those who
tres - pass a - gainst us; and lead us not in - to temp-ta-tion,
but de - liv - er us from e -vil.

159 *The Lord's Prayer 2*

Our Fa - ther who art in heav- en, hal - lowed be thy name;
thy king - dom come; thy will be done on earth as it
is in heav-en. Give us this day our dai - ly bread;
and for - give us our tres - pass - es as we for-give those who
tres - pass a - gainst us; and lead us not in - to temp-ta - tion,
but de - liv - er us from e - vil.

Doxology after the Lord's Prayer

160 *For the Kingdom 1*

E.A.C.

For the king - dom, the power, and the glo - ry are
yours, now and for - ev - er.

161 *For the Kingdom 2*

E.A.C.

For the king - dom, the power, and the glo - ry are
yours, now and for - ev - er.

Lamb of God 1

Lamb of God, you take a - way the sins of the world, have
mer - cy on us. Lamb of God, you take a - way the
sins of the world, have mer - cy on us. Lamb of God, you
take a - way the sins of the world, grant us peace.

Lamb of God 2

Lamb of God, you take a - way the sins of the world, have
mer - cy on us.
Lamb of God, you take a - way the
sins of the world, have mer - cy on us.
Lamb of
God, you take a - way the sins of the world, grant us peace.

Lamb of God 3

Lamb of God, you take a-way the sins of the world, have
mer-cy on us. Lamb of God, you take a-way the sins of the
world, have mer-cy on us. Lamb of God, you
take a-way the sins of the world, grant us peace.

Lamb of God 4

Lamb of God, you take a - way the sins of the world, have mer - cy on us.
Lamb of God, you take a - way the sins of the world, have mer - cy on us.
Lamb of God, you take a - way the sins of the world, grant us peace.

166 *O Saving Victim*

O Salutaris

Abbe Duguet 18th century

1. O sav - ing Vic - tim, o - pen wide
2. To thy great name be end - less praise,
The gate of heav'n to man be - low,
Im - mor - tal God - head, One in Three,
Our foes press on from ev - 'ry side;
Oh, grant us end - less length of days,
Thine aid sup - ply; thy strength be - stow.
In our true na - tive land with Thee. A - men.

167 *Humbly Let Us Voice Our Homage*

Tantum Ergo

Casper Ett, 1840

1. Hum-bly let us voice our hom - age For so great a sac - ra - ment:
2. Glo - ry, hon - or, ad - o - ra - tion Let us sing with one ac - cord!
1. Let all for - mer rites sur - ren - der To the Lord's New Test - a - ment;
2. Praised be God, al- might - y Fa - ther; Praised be Christ, his Son, our Lord;
What our sen - ses fail to fath-om Let us grasp thru faith's consent.
Praised be God the Ho - ly Spir - it; Tri - une God-head be a-dored. A - men.

Priest: You have given them bread from heaven (Alleluia).
People: Having all sweetness within it (Alleluia).

168 *The Small Child Sings*

Sister M. Margaret

The small child sings on his way to God
1. When he wakes up in the morning: "Good morning, God."
2. When he splashes in the water: "It's lovely, God."
3. Before he eats his food: "Oh, thank You, God."

4. The small child sings on his way to God
When he looks up at the stars:
"You're great, God."

5. The small child sings on his way to God
When he goes to bed at night:
"Good night, God."

169 *I'm So Glad*

Sister M. Margaret

I'm so glad God is with me all the day,__(repeat) When I
I'm so glad God is with me all the night,__(repeat) When my
work and when I pray, When I laugh and sing and play. I'm so glad God is with me all the day.
mo-ther hugs me tight, And then switches off the light, I'm so glad God is with me all the night.

170 *When I Was Baptized*

Sister M. Margaret

When I was bap-tised, I re-ceived God's gift, His life and love in me;
One day He will say: "Come home to Me, Come home to heav'n with Me."

171 *In Praise of God*

Sister M. Margaret

1. You set the plan - ets spin-ning up so high, You set the
2. You set the waves a - crash-ing on the sand, You set the
3. You set the birds a - sing-ing in the trees, You set the
sun a - shining in the sky;
things a - grow-ing on the land;
plants a - nodding in the breeze;
With a mind to know, And a heart to
love; I thank You, God my Fa - ther.

4. You set the bees a-humming in the flowers,
You set the rainbow gleaming through the showers;
With a mind to know, and a heart to love,
I thank You, God my Father.

5. You set the people on your lovely earth,
You set them here and told them of their worth;
With a mind to know, and a heart to love,
I thank You, God my Father.

6. You set each one of us upon our way,
For You want us to be with You some day;
With a mind to know, and a heart to love,
I thank You, God my Father.

172 *Jesus, Love Is in Your Heart*

Sister M. Margaret

Je - sus, love is in Your Heart For Your Fa - ther and for men;
Let us share this great love, As we live Your life. A - men.

173 *Jesus, on the Cross You Died*

Sister M. Margaret

1. Je - sus, on the cross You died, Died, but then You came a - live, A-
2. Now You share this life with me, Share this life that I may be,
live with a new and ris - en life, Al - le - lu - ia!
Filled with love for God and men, Al - le - lu - ia!

174 *Our Giving-to-God Song*

Sister M. Margaret

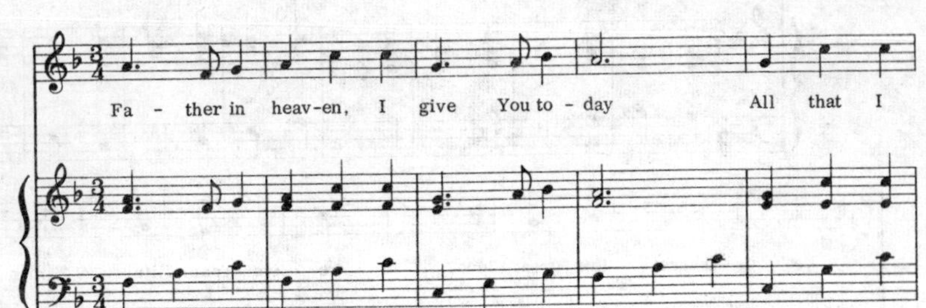
Fa - ther in heav-en, I give You to - day All that I

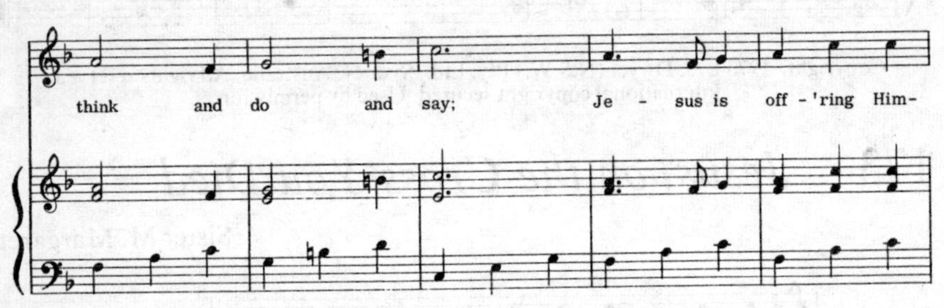
think and do and say; Je - sus is off - 'ring Him-

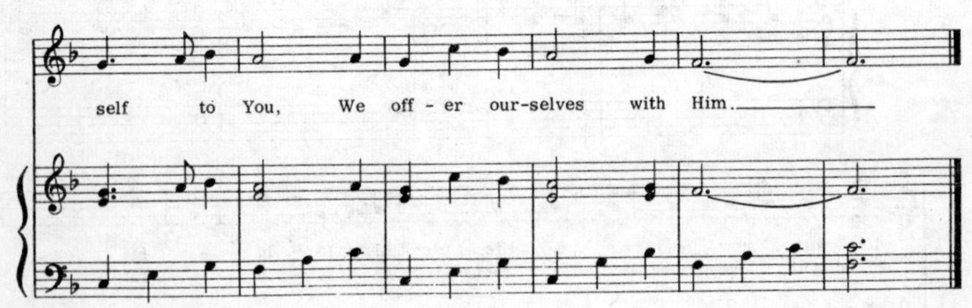
self to You, We off - er our-selves with Him.

175 *The Small Child Pays a Visit*

Sister M. Margaret

Je - sus, I'm in Your house, And I'd like to say;
Hel - lo and I love You, Teach me how to pray.

176 *The Small Child Makes His Own Prayer*

Sister M. Margaret

I join my hands and I bow my head, And I speak to God my Fa - ther.

177 *We Pray for Our Priest*

Sister M. Margaret

God bless our Priest and help___ him to do his work each day;

As he leads God's peo-ple___ Up-on their Heav'nly way.
May he be like Je-sus___ His

Lead-er strong and true;
As he loves our Fa-ther___ And all God's peo-ple, too.

178 *The Small Child Prays for Others*

Sister M. Margaret

Let us ask God to bless our mo-thers and our fa-thers! Make them

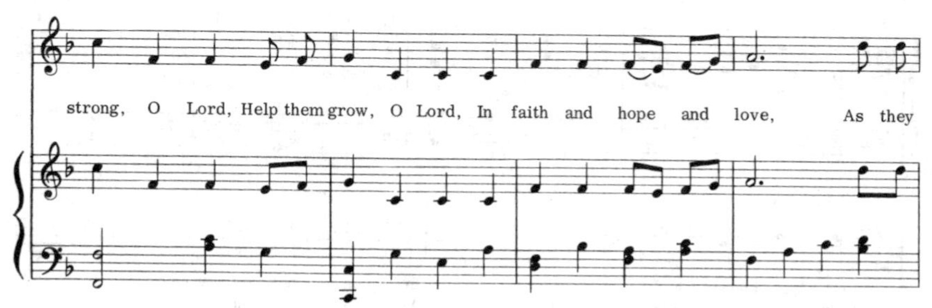
strong, O Lord, Help them grow, O Lord, In faith and hope and love, As they

pray, O Lord, as they work, O Lord, On their way to You a - bove.

179 *God Gives Us an Angel*

Sister M. Margaret

1. To help us on our way to Him, God gave each girl and boy, An
2. Dear an-gel, you are with me, To help me on my way,
an-gel strong and beaut-i-ful, He wor-ships God with joy. An
As I try to love God, And please Him more each day;
an-gel knows and loves God In an an-gel way, And
Help me to love oth-ers As I work and play;
he will help us know God, And please Him more each day.
Then I'll please my Fa-ther And show my love each day.

180 *Mary, My Mother*

Sister M. Margaret

1. Ma - ry my Mo - ther, I love you, I talk to you
2. Teach me to talk to my Fa - ther And tell Him that

ev - 'ry day; Ma - ry my Mo - ther, please
He is so good; Help me to love all my

help me As I walk a - long my way.
play - mates As I know a lit - tle child should.

181 *Dear Saint Joseph*

Sister M. Margaret

Dear Saint Jo - seph, We your child - ren Ask your help to - day.
We want to please Our Lov - ing Fa - ther In all we do and think and say.

182 *Going Home Song*

Sister M. Margaret

Thank You for this hap - py day, For all our work and all our play;
Guard us on our home-ward way, God our Lov - ing Fa - ther.

183

A Child's Prayer

Carol McAfee Morgan — Anon. From "Lieder Perien . . ." 1894

mp
1. Dear God, may I be brave — to - day, And
2. If there is some - one now — in — need Of
3. As I grow up I give — to — Thee All
mp
do my best in ev - 'ry — way. May I not shirk — the —
gen - tle word or thought - ful — deed, Show me Thy will — And —
that I am and all — I'll — be. Thou art my friend, Show —
mf
small - est — task, Nor fear the big — ones. — This — I — ask.
help me — use Thy way of kind - ness. — This — I — choose.
me Thy — way of lov - ing ser - vice. — This — I — pray.
mf

184 *Prayer before We Eat*

Sister M. Margaret

When it is time to eat my food, I like to stop and say;
Thank — You, God, for plan - ning This good food for me to - day.

185 *Prayer after We Eat*

Sister M. Margaret

Thank You for our food, And would You kind - ly bless, The
peo - ple who pre-pared it, And give them hap - pi - ness.

186 *The Small Child Prays for His country*

Sister M. Margaret

Our flag is fly - ing up so high, I love the red and white and blue, May
God pro-tect Am - er - i - ca And keep us ev - er true.

187 *The Small Child Checks Up at Night*

Sister M. Margaret

Be - fore I go to bed each night I close my eyes and say;
Fa - ther help me to find out How I loved You all the day.

ADDITIONAL HYMNS

for various occasions

188 *Alas! And Did My Savior Bleed?*

Isaac Watts

Hugh Wilson

1. A - las! and did my — Sav - iour bleed? And
2. Was it for crimes that — I have done He
3. Well might the sun in — dark - ness hide, And
4. But drops of grief can — ne'er re - pay The
did my — Sov - 'reign die? Would He de - vote that
groaned up - on the tree? A - maz - ing pit - y!
shut his — glo - ries in, When Christ, the might - y
debt of — love I owe; Here, Lord, I give my -
sa - cred head For such — worm as I?
grace un - known! And love be - yond de - gree!
Mak - er, died For man, the — crea - ture's sin.
self a - way 'Tis all that — I can do.

189

Abide with Me

W. H. Monk

1. A - bide with me! fast falls the e - ven - tide;
2. Swift to its close ebbs out life's lit - tle day;
3. I need Thy pres - ence ev - ery pass - ing hour,
4. I fear no foe, with Thee at hand to bless;
The dark - ness thick - ens, Lord, with me a - bide;
Earth's joys grow dim; its glo - ries pass a - way:
What but Thy grace can foil the temp - ter's power?
Ills have no weight, and tears no bit - ter - ness:
When oth - er help - ers fail, and com - forts flee,
Change and de - cay in all a - round I see;
Who like Thy - self my guide and stay can be?
Where is death's sting? where, grave, thy vic - to - ry?
Help of the help - less, oh, a - bide with me!
O Thou, Who chang - est not, a - bide with me!
Through cloud and sun - shine, oh, a - bide with me!
I tri - umph still, if Thou a - bide with me!

190 *Angels, from the Realms of Glory*

James Montgomery

Henry Smart

mp

1. An-gels, from the realms of glo - ry, Wing your flight o'er all the earth;
2. Shep-herds, in the field a - bid - ing, Watch - ing o'er your flocks by night,
3. Sa - ges, leave your con - tem-pla-tions, Bright - er vi - sions beam a - far;
4. Saints, be - fore the al - tar bend-ing, Watch - ing long in hope and fear,
5. Sin - ners,wrung with true re - pent-ance,Doomed for guilt to end - less pains,

Ye whc sang cre - a - tion's sto - ry, Now pro-claim Mes - si - ah's birth:
God with man is _ now re - sid - ing; Yon - der shines the in - fant light:
Seek the great De - sire of na - tions; Ye have seen His na - tal star:
Sud - den - ly the _ Lord, de - scend - ing, In His tem - ple shall ap - pear:
Jus - tice now re - vokes the sen - tence, Mer - cy calls you, break your chains:

Come and wor - ship, come and wor - ship, Wor - ship Christ, the new born King.

191 *All People That on Earth Do Dwell*

William Kethe

Genevan Psalter

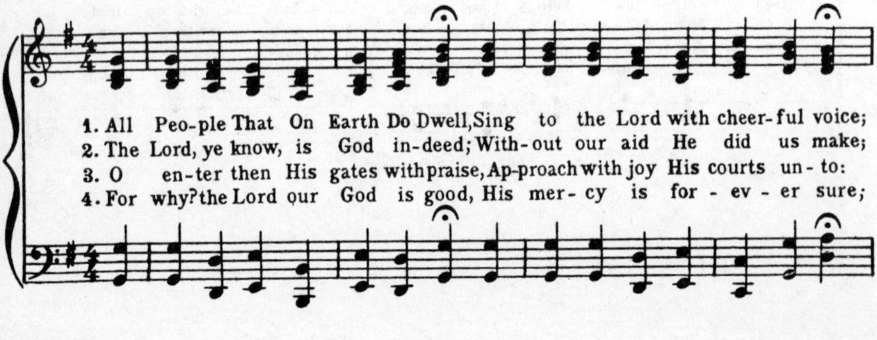

1. All Peo - ple That On Earth Do Dwell,Sing to the Lord with cheer - ful voice;
2. The Lord, ye know, is God in - deed; With - out our aid He did us make;
3. O en - ter then His gates with praise, Ap - proach with joy His courts un - to:
4. For why? the Lord our God is good, His mer - cy is for - ev - er sure;

Him serve with fear, His praise forth tell; Come ye be-fore Him and re-joice.
We are His flock, He doth us feed, And for His sheep He doth us take.
Praise, laud, and bless His name al-ways, For it is seem-ly so to do.
His truth at all times firm-ly stood, And shall from age to age en-dure.

192 *My God, How Wonderful*

Father Faber

Mendelssohn

1. My God! how wonderful Thou art, Thy majesty how bright,

How beautiful Thy Mercy seat, In depths of burning light!

2. Oh how I fear Thee, living God!
With deepest, tenderest fears,
And worship Thee with trembling hope,
And penitential tears.

3. Oh then this worse than worthless heart
In pity deign to take,
And make it love Thee, for Thyself,
And for Thy glory's sake.

4. No earthly father loves like Thee,
No mother half so mild
Bears and forbears, as Thou hast done,
With me, Thy sinful child.

193 *Good King Wenceslas*

Ancient Carol

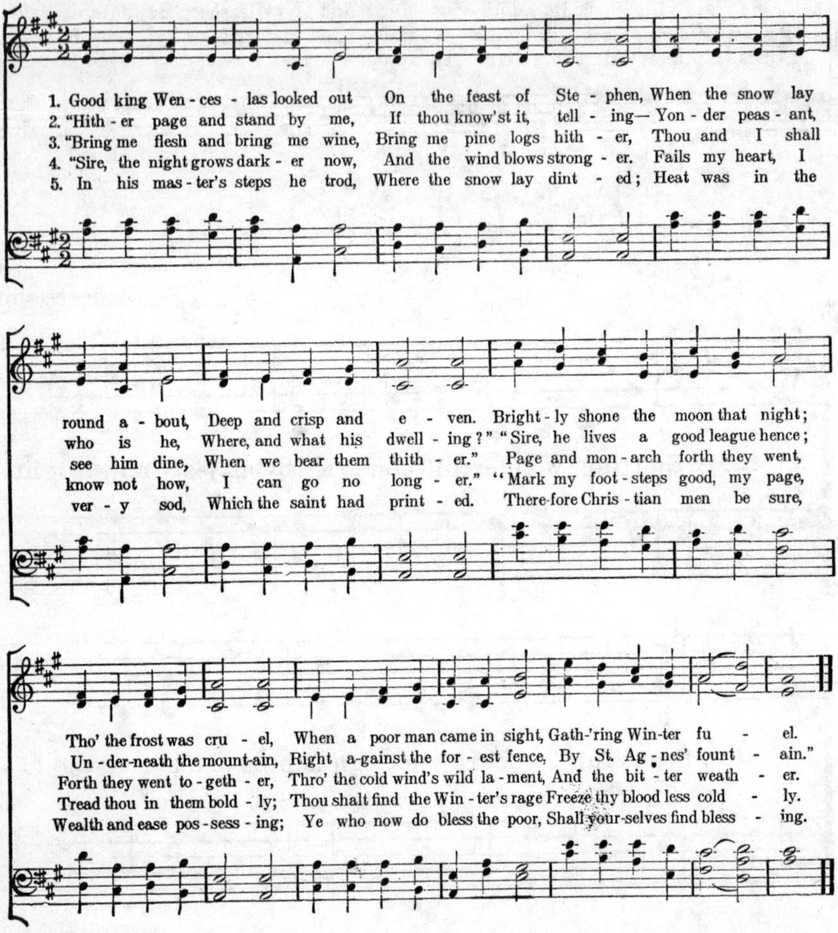

1. Good king Wen - ces - las looked out On the feast of Ste - phen, When the snow lay
2. "Hith - er page and stand by me, If thou know'st it, tell - ing— Yon - der peas - ant,
3. "Bring me flesh and bring me wine, Bring me pine logs hith - er, Thou and I shall
4. "Sire, the night grows dark - er now, And the wind blows strong - er. Fails my heart, I
5. In his mas - ter's steps he trod, Where the snow lay dint - ed; Heat was in the

round a - bout, Deep and crisp and e - ven. Bright - ly shone the moon that night;
who is he, Where, and what his dwell - ing?" "Sire, he lives a good league hence;
see him dine, When we bear them thith - er." Page and mon - arch forth they went,
know not how, I can go no long - er." "Mark my foot - steps good, my page,
ver - y sod, Which the saint had print - ed. There-fore Chris - tian men be sure,

Tho' the frost was cru - el, When a poor man came in sight, Gath-'ring Win-ter fu - el.
Un - der-neath the mount-ain, Right a-gainst the for - est fence, By St. Ag - nes' fount - ain."
Forth they went to - geth - er, Thro' the cold wind's wild la - ment, And the bit - ter weath - er.
Tread thou in them bold - ly; Thou shalt find the Win - ter's rage Freeze thy blood less cold - ly.
Wealth and ease pos - sess - ing; Ye who now do bless the poor, Shall your-selves find bless - ing.

194 *Away in a Manger*

Martin Luther

Herbert Griggs

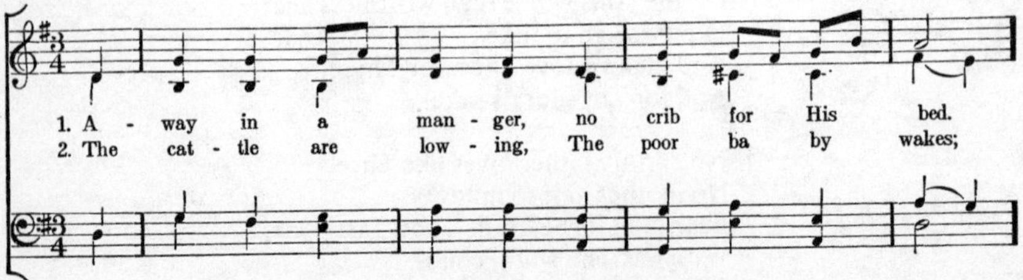
1. A - way in a man - ger, no crib for His bed.
2. The cat - tle are low - ing, The poor ba by wakes;

The in - fant Lord Je - sus, Lay down His sweet head.
But lit - tle Lord Je - sus, No cry - ing He makes.
The stars in the sky, Looked down where He lay.
I love Thee, Lord, Je - sus, Look down from the sky.
The in - fant, Lord, Je - sus, A - sleep in the hay.
And stay by my side, Till the day - light is nigh.

195 *Art Thou Weary*

John W. Neale, 1862 — Henry W. Baker, 1862

1. Art thou wea - ry, art thou lan - guid, Art thou sore dis - tressed?
2. Hath he marks to lead me to him, If he be my Guide?
3. Is there di - a - dem, as Mon - arch, That his brow a - dorns?

'Come to me,' saith One, 'and com - ing, Be at __ rest.'
'In his feet and hands are wound-prints, And his __ side.'
'Yea, a crown, in ver - y sure - ty; But of __ thorns.'

196 *Lord God of Morning*

John Keble

"Germany." From Beethoven

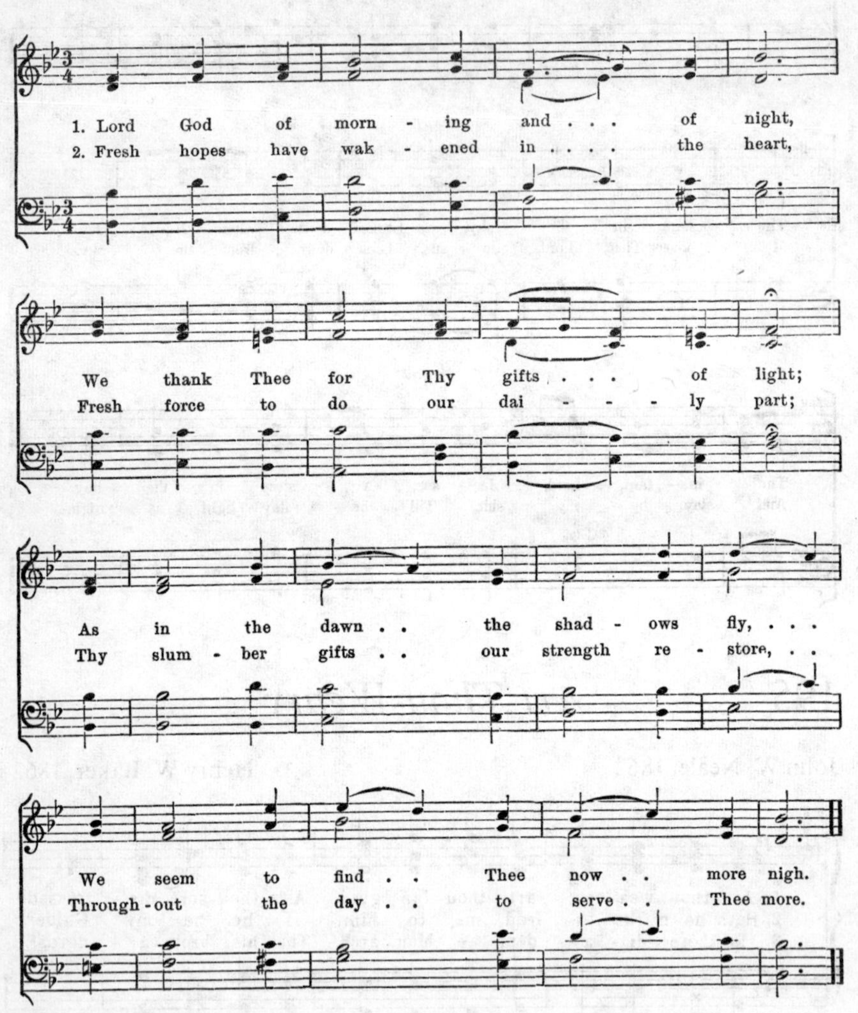
1. Lord God of morn - ing and . . . of night,
2. Fresh hopes have wak - ened in . . . the heart,
We thank Thee for Thy gifts . . . of light;
Fresh force to do our dai - - ly part;
As in the dawn . . the shad - ows fly, . . .
Thy slum - ber gifts . . our strength re - store, . .
We seem to find . . Thee now . . more nigh.
Through - out the day . . to serve . . Thee more.

3. O Lord of light, 'tis Thou alone
Canst make our darkened hearts Thine own;
O then be with us, Lord, that we
In Thy great day may wake to Thee.

4. Praise God, our Maker and our Friend;
Praise Him through time, till time shall end;
Till psalm and song His name adore,
Through Heaven's great day of evermore.

197 *Now the Day Is Over*

Sabine Baring-Gould

J. Barnby

1. Now the day is . . . o - - - ver,
2. Now the dark - - ness gath - - - ers,
Night is draw - ing nigh, ...
Stars be - gin to peep, ...
Shad - ows of the ev'n - - ing
Birds and beasts, and flow - - ers
Steal a - cross the sky.
Soon will be a - sleep.
A - - MEN.

3. Jesus, give the weary
   Calm and sweet repose,
   With Thy tenderest blessing
   May our eyelids close.

4. Grant to little children
   Visions bright of Thee,
   Guard the sailors tossing
   On the deep blue sea.

5. Comfort every sufferer
   Watching late in pain,
   Those who plan some evil
   From their sin restrain.

6. Through the long night
   watches
   May Thine angels spread
   Their white wings above me,
   Watching round my bed.

7. When the morning wakens,
   Then may I arise
   Pure and fresh and sinless
   In Thy holy eyes.

8. Glory to the Father,
   Glory to the Son,
   And to Thee, blest Spirit,
   Whilst all ages run. Amen.

198 *As the Dewy Shades of Even*

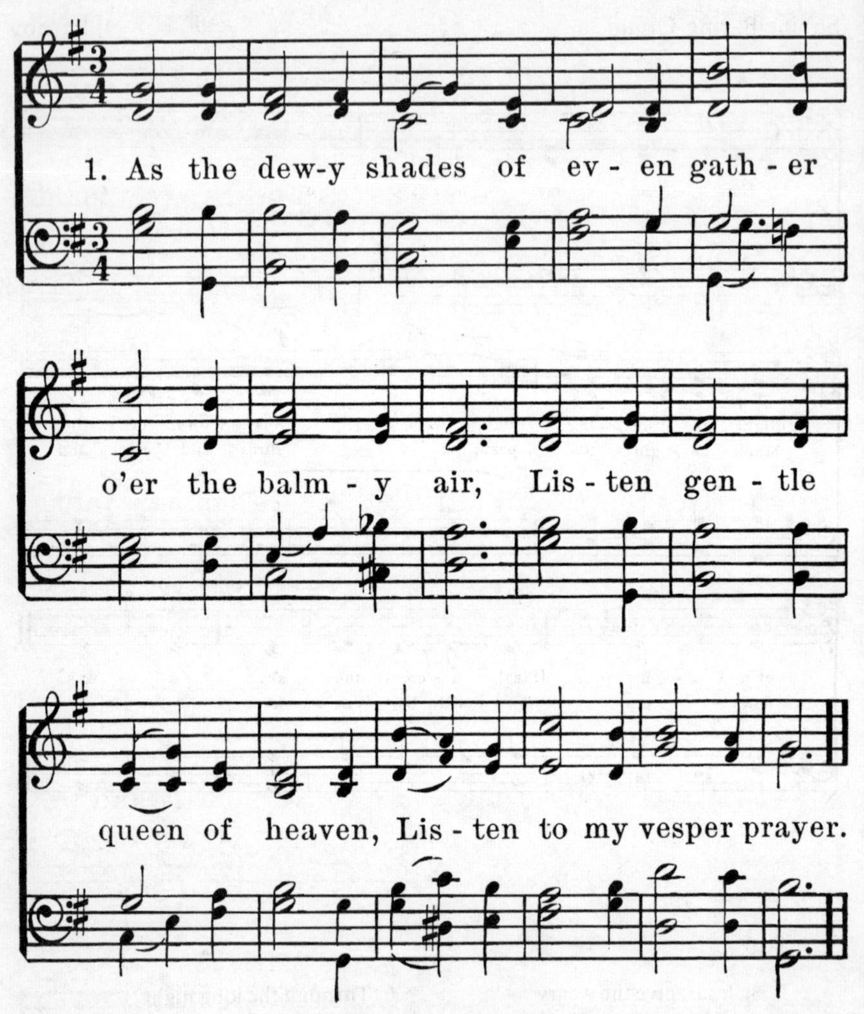
1. As the dew-y shades of ev - en gath - er
o'er the balm - y air, Lis - ten gen - tle
queen of heaven, Lis - ten to my vesper prayer.

2. Holy Mother, near me hover,
Free my thoughts from aught defiled,
With thy wings of mercy cover,
Keep from sin thy helpless child.

3. Thine own sinless heart was broken,
Sorrow's sword had pierced its core;
Holy Mother, by that token,
Now thy pity I implore.

199 O Purest of Creatures

Father Faber

Adapted from an old melody

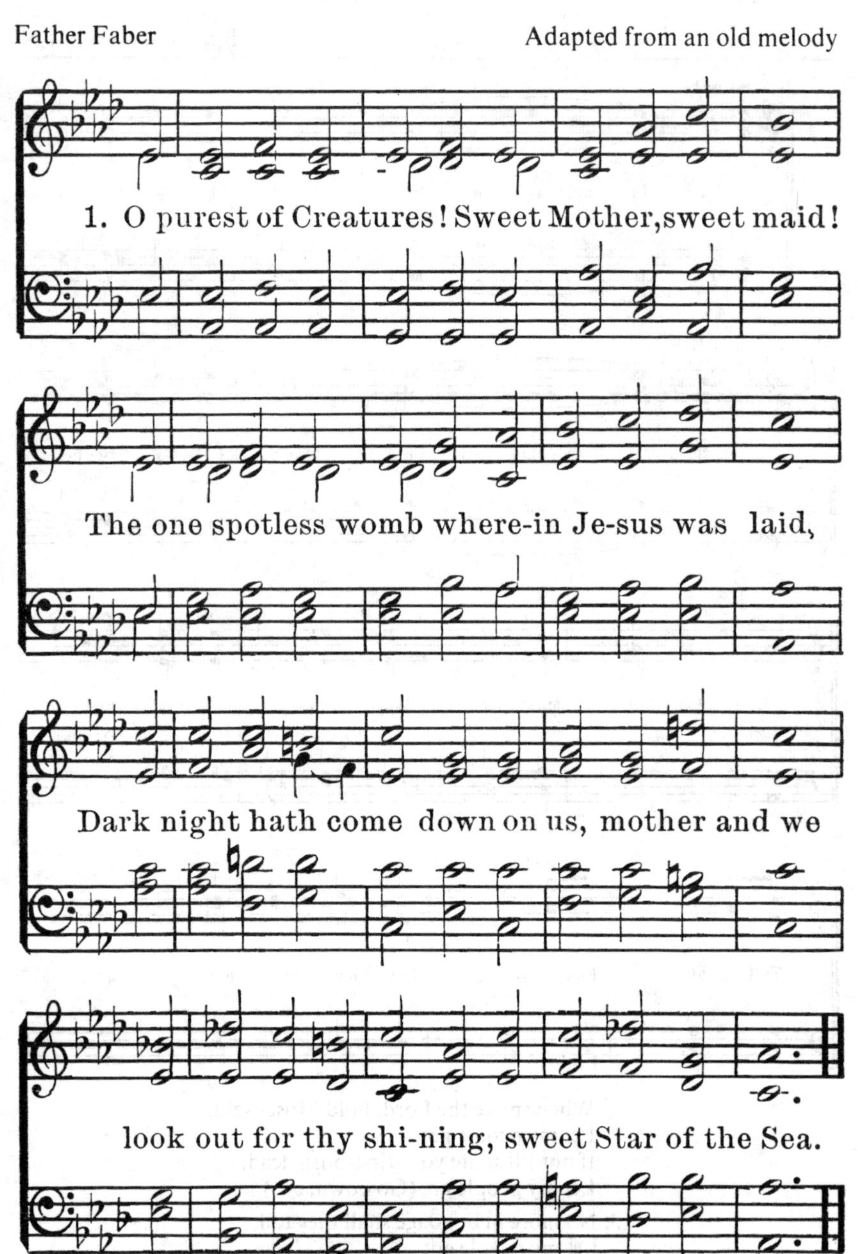

1. O purest of Creatures! Sweet Mother, sweet maid!
The one spotless womb where-in Je-sus was laid,
Dark night hath come down on us, mother and we
look out for thy shi-ning, sweet Star of the Sea.

200 Go Down, Moses

Spiritual Arr. R.J.N.

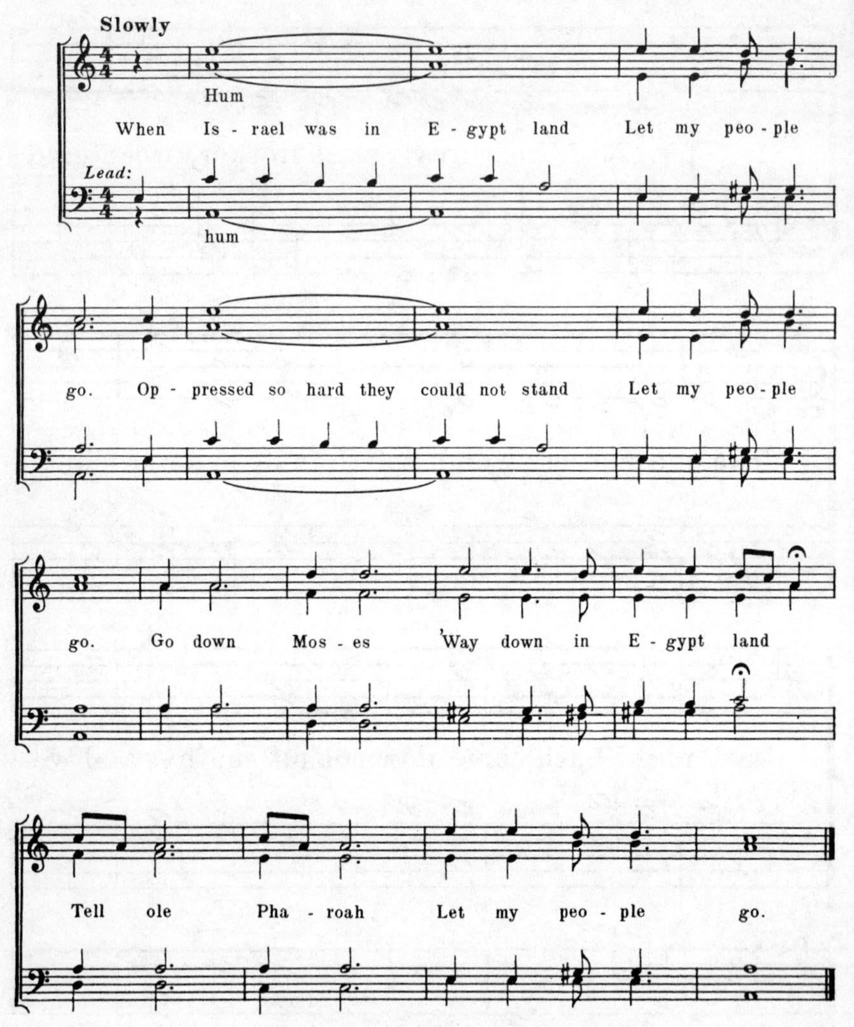
Slowly
Hum
When Is - rael was in E - gypt land Let my peo - ple
Lead:
hum
go. Op - pressed so hard they could not stand Let my peo - ple
go. Go down Mos - es 'Way down in E - gypt land
Tell ole Pha - roah Let my peo - ple go.

2. When spoke the Lord, bold Moses said,
   Let my people go;
   If not I'll smite your first-born dead,
   Let my people go. (Go down, etc.)
3. No more in bondage shall they toil,
   Let my people go;
   Let them come out with Israel's soil,
   Let my people go. (Go down, etc.)

201 *Nobody Knows the Trouble I've Seen*

Spiritual Arr. R.J.N.

CHORUS
Slowly
No-bod - y knows the trou-ble I've seen, No-bod - y knows but Je - sus,
Hum
No-bod - y knows the trou-ble I've seen, Glo - ry Hal - le - lu - jah.
VERSE
Some - times I'm up, some - times I'm down, Yes! Yes! Lord! Some -
times I'm al - most to the ground, Yes! Yes! Lord.

2. Oh, every day to you I pray,
Oh, yes, Lord.
For you to drive my sins away,
Oh, yes, Lord.

202 *Heart of Mary*

1. Heart of Ma - ry, heart the pur - est, Ev - er shrined in mor - tal frame, Blest a - sy - lum who se - cur - est, All who thy pro - tec - tion

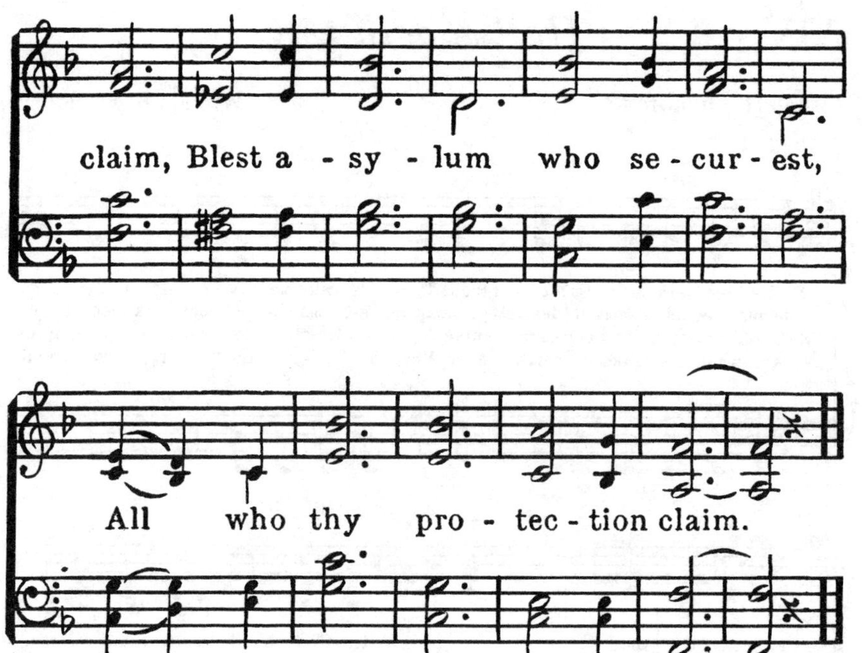
claim, Blest a - sy - lum who se - cur - est,
All who thy pro - tec - tion claim.

2. Hear the prayer of one whose weakness,
Most demands a mother's care;
: One to whom thy looks, all meekness,
Counsel hope, forbid despair.:

3. To some spot where ne'er might hover
Danger's shadows I would flee;
: Ah! but where that spot discover,
Where, ah! Mary, but in thee.:

203 *He Leadeth Me*

Joseph H. Gilmore | William B. Bradbury

1. He lead-eth me! O bless-ed tho't! O words with heav'n-ly com-fort fraught! What-
2. Sometimes 'mid scenes of deep-est gloom, Sometimes where E-den's bow-ers bloom, By
3. Lord, I would clasp Thy hand in mine, Nor ever mur-mur nor re-pine, Con-
4. And when my task on earth is done, When, by Thy grace, the vic-try's won, E'en
e'er I do, wher-e'er I be, Still 'tis God's hand that lead-eth me.
wa-ters still, o'er troub-led sea, Still 'tis His hand that lead-eth me!
tent, what-ev-er lot I see, Since 'tis my God that lead-eth me!
death's cold wave I will not flee, Since God thro' Jor-dan lead-eth me.
Refrain
He lead-eth me, He lead-eth me, By His own hand He lead-eth me: His
faith ful fol-lower I would be, For by His hand He lead-eth me.

204 *I Need Thee Every Hour*

Annie S. Hawks

Robert Lowry

1. I need Thee ev-'ry hour, Most gra - cious Lord; No ten - der voice like Thine Can peace af - ford.
2. I need Thee ev-'ry hour, Stay Thou near by; Temp - ta - tions lose their pow'r When Thou art nigh.
3. I need Thee ev-'ry hour, In joy or pain; Come quick - ly and a - bide, Or life is vain.
4. I need Thee ev-'ry hour, Most Ho - ly One; O make me Thine in - deed, Thou bless - ed Son!
Chorus
I need Thee, O I need Thee; Ev-'ry hour I need Thee; O bless me now, my Sav - iour, I come to Thee!

205 *Holy Patron*

Chorus.
1. Ho-ly pa - tron thee sa - lut - ing,
Here we meet with hearts sin - cere, Blest St.
Jo - seph all u - nit - ing, Call on
thee to hear our prayer. Happy saint in bliss a -

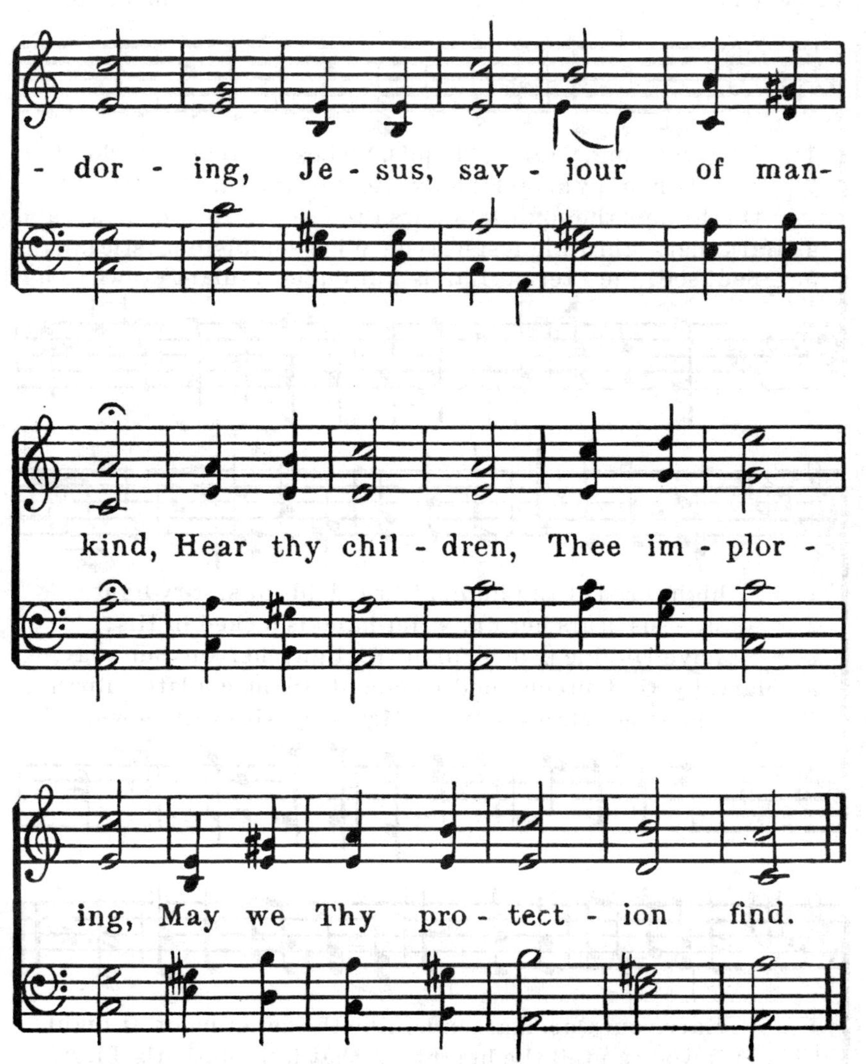
- dor - ing, Je - sus, sav - iour of man-
kind, Hear thy chil - dren, Thee im - plor -
ing, May we Thy pro - tect - ion find.

2. Worldly dangers for them fearing
Youthful hearts to thee we bring;
Grant, in virtue persevering,
Vice may ne'er their bosoms sting.

206 *Hymn of the Angels*

Father Faber
Old Catholic Melody
1. Sing, sing, ye an-gel bands, All beautiful and bright; For
2. O hap-py an-gels! look, How beautiful she is! See
3. On through the countless stars Proceeds the bright array; and
4. Hark! hark! thro' highest heaven What sounds of mystic mirth!
5. See! see! the Eternal Hands Put on her radiant crown, And
1 high-er still and higher Thro' fields of star-ry light,
2 Je-sus bears her up, Her hand is locked in His;
3 Love Di-vine comes forth To light her on her way,
4 Mary, by God proclaimed Queen of Im-mac-u-late Birth,
5 the sweet Majes-ty Of Mer-cy sit-teth down,
1 Mary, your Queen, ascends, Like the sweet moon at night.
2 Oh who can tell the height Of that fair Mother's bliss?
3 Through the short gloom of night, In-to ce-les-tial day.
4 And diademed with stars, The lowliest of the earth!
5 For ev-er and for ever, On her pre-destin-ed throne.

207 *Hymn to the Pope*

Gounod

Vi - va . . . ., padre nos-tro e Pa - pa!
al nos-tro a - mo-re lo con-ser vi il cie - lo! . .
Vi - va. . . . . . . , pa-dre nos-tro e Pa - pa!
lo con-ser-vi al nos-tro a-mor il Cie - lo.

208 *See the Paraclete*

Russian Air
1. See the Par-a-clete descending, Burning with ce-
les-tial fire; Grace and truth on Him at-tend-ing,
Men with heavn'ly love inspire, Let us Al - le -
He all heavn'ly
lu - ia sing-ing, Of - fer him our grateful lays.
gra-ces bringing, Mer-its ev - er-last-ing praise.

209 *Jesus, Lover of My Soul*

Charles Wesley

Simeon B. Marsh

1. Je - sus, Lov - er of my soul, Let me to Thy bos - om fly,
2. Oth - er ref - uge have I none; Hangs my help - less soul on Thee;
3. Thou, O Christ, art all I want; More than all in Thee I find;
4. Plen-teous grace with Thee is found, Grace to cov - er all my sin;
While the near - er wa - ters roll, While the tem - pest still is high.
Leave, ah, leave me not a - lone, Still sup - port and com - fort me.
Raise the fall - en, cheer the faint, Heal the sick, and lead the blind.
Let the heal - ing streams a - bound; Make and keep me pure with - in.
Hide me, O my Sav - iour, hide, Till the storm of life is past;
All my trust on Thee is stayed, All my help from Thee I bring;
Just and ho - ly is Thy name, I am all un - right - eous - ness;
Thou of life the Foun-tain art, Free - ly let me take of Thee;
Safe in - to the ha - ven guide, O re - ceive my soul at last!
Cov - er my de - fense-less head With the shad - ow of Thy wing.
Vile and full of sin I am, Thou art full of truth and grace.
Spring Thou up with - in my heart, Rise to all e - ter - ni - ty.

210 *Nearer My God to Thee*

Sarah F. Adams

Lowell Mason

1. Near- er, my God, to Thee, Near - er to Thee E'en tho' it be a cross
2. Tho' like a wan-der-er, The sun gone down, Dark-ness be o - ver me,
3. There let the way ap-pear Steps un - to heav'n; All that Thou send-est me,
4. Or, if on joy-ful wing, Cleav - ing the sky, Sun, moon, and stars for-got,

That rais-eth me; Still all my song shall be, Near-er, my God, to Thee.
My rest a stone; Yet in my dreams I'd be, Near-er, my God, to Thee.
In mer-cy giv'n; An-gels to beck - on me Near - er, my God, to Thee.
Up-ward I fly; Still all my song shall be, Near-er, my God, to Thee.

Near - er, my God, to Thee, Near - er to Thee.

211 *Our God, Our Help*

Isaac Watts

William Croft

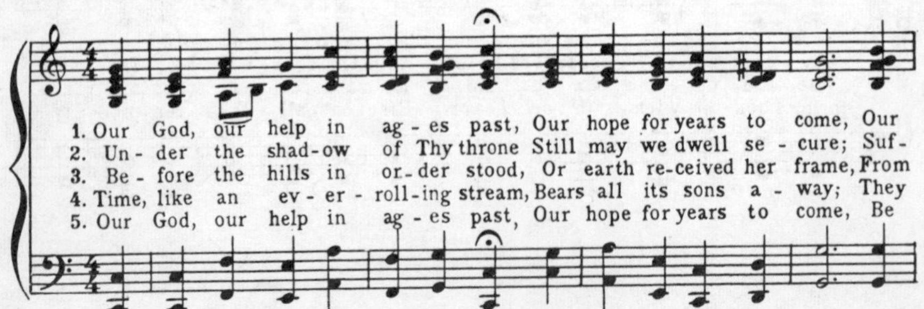
1. Our God, our help in ag - es past, Our hope for years to come, Our
2. Un - der the shad - ow of Thy throne Still may we dwell se - cure; Suf-
3. Be - fore the hills in or - der stood, Or earth re-ceived her frame, From
4. Time, like an ev - er - roll - ing stream, Bears all its sons a - way; They
5. Our God, our help in ag - es past, Our hope for years to come, Be

shel - ter from the storm - y blast, And our e - ter - nal home!
fi - cient is Thine arm a - lone, And our de - fense is sure.
ev - er - last - ing Thou art God, To end - less years the same.
fly, for - got - ten, as a dream Dies at the ope - ning day.
Thou our guide while life shall last, And our e - ter - nal home!

212 *Lead, Kindly Light*

John H. Newman

John B. Dykes

1. Lead, kind - ly Light, a - mid th'en - cir - cling gloom, Lead Thou me
2. I was not ev - er thus, nor prayed that Thou Shouldst lead me
3. So long Thy power hath blest me, sure it still Will lead me

on; The night is dark, and I am far from home; Lead Thou me
on; I loved to choose and see my path; but now Lead Thou me
on, O'er moor and fen, o'er crag and tor - rent, till The night is

on: Keep Thou my feet; I do not ask to
on. I loved the gar - ish day, and, spite of
gone; And with the morn those an - gel fac - es

see The dis - tant scene one step e - nough for me.
fears, Pride ruled my will: re - mem - ber not past years.
smile, Which I have loved long since, and lost a - while.

Jesus My Lord, My God

Father Faber

Haydn

1. Je - sus my Lord, my God, my all!
How can I love Thee as I ought?
And how re-vere this won-drous gift,
So far sur - pass - ing hope or thought?

Sweet Sac - ra - ment: we Thee a - dore!
O make us love Thee, more and more.

2. O earth! grow flowers beneath His feet,
And thou, O sun, shine bright this day!
He comes! He comes! Oh, heaven on earth
Our Jesus comes upon His Way!
Sweet Sacrament! we Thee adore!
Oh, make us love Thee more and more!

3. He comes! He comes! The Lord of Hosts,
Borne on His throne triumphantly!
We see Thee, and we know Thee, Lord,
And yearn to shed our blood for Thee.
Sweet Sacrament! we Thee adore!
Oh, make us love Thee more and more!

214 *When Evening Shades Are Falling*

Thomas Moore, 1825

1. When evening shades are falling O'er ocean's sunny
sleep, To pil-grims heart re - call-ing, Their
home be - yond the deep; When rest o'er all de-
scend-ing, The shores with gladness smile, And

lutes, their echoes blending Are heard from isle to isle.
CHORUS.
Then Mary, Mother Mary, Thou bright star of the sea,
We'll pray to thee our Mother, We'll pray, we'll pray to thee.

2. The noonday tempest over,
Now ocean toils no more,
And wings of halcyons hover,
Where all was strife before.
Oh! thus my life, in closing,
Its short tempestuous day,
Beneath heav'n's smile reposing,
Shine all its storms away.

215 *We Thank Thee, O Our Father*

Anonymous

1. We thank Thee, O our Fa - ther, For all thy lov - ing care;– We
2. Out in the sun - ny mead - ows, And in the wood - lands cool,– Up -
3. And in the dust - y cit - y, Where bus - y crowds pass by, — And
4. And wheth - er in the cit - y, Or in the fields they dwell;– Al -
thank Thee that thou mad - est The world so bright and fair. – We
on the breez - y hill - side, And by each reed - y pool,– And
where the tall dark hous - es Stand up and hide the sky, — And
ways the same sweet mes - sage The fair sweet flow - ers tell. – For
thank Thee for the sun - shine, And for the pleas - ant show'rs; And
in the qui - et pas - ture, And by the broad high - way;– All
where through lanes and al - leys No pleas - ant breez - es blow,– E'en
they are all so won - der - ful, They show thy pow'r a - broad;– And
O, our God, we thank Thee, We thank Thee for the flow'rs.
pure, and fresh, and stain - less, They spring up ev - 'ry day. —
there, O God our Fa - ther Thou mak'st the flow - ers grow. –
they are all so beau - ti - ful, They tell Thy love, O God. —

216 *Rock of Ages*

Augustus M. Toplady
Thomas Hastings
1. Rock of Ag - es cleft for me, Let me hide my- self in
2. Could my tears for - ev - er flow, Could my zeal no lan - guor
3. While I draw this fleet-ing breath, When my eyes shall close in
Thee; Let the wa - ter and the blood, From Thy wound - ed side which
know, These for sin could not a - tone; Thou must save, and Thou a -
death, When I rise to worlds un - known, And be - hold Thee on Thy
flowed, Be of sin the dou-ble cure, Save from wrath and make me pure.
lone: In my hand no price I bring, Sim - ply to Thy cross I cling.
throne Rock of Ag - es, cleft for me, Let me hide my-self in Thee.
217 Pass Me Not
Fanny J. Crosby
William H. Doane
1. Pass me not, O gen - tle Sav- iour, Hear my hum-ble cry,
2. Let me at a throne of mer - cy Find a sweet re - lief;
3. Trust - ing on - ly in Thy mer - it, Would I seek Thy face;
4. Thou the Spring of all my com - fort, More than life to me,
While on oth - ers Thou art call - ing, Do not pass me by.
Kneel-ing there in deep con - tri - tion, Help my un - be - lief.
Heal my wound-ed, bro - ken spir - it, Save me by Thy grace.
Whom have I on earth be - side Thee? Whom in heav'n but Thee?

218 *When Morning Gilds the Skies*

Rev. E. Caswell | Joseph Barnby

1. When morn-ing gilds the skies, My heart a-wak-ing
2. Does sad-ness fill my mind, A sol-ace here I
3. In heav'ns e-ter-nal bliss The love-liest strain is
4. Be this, while life is mine, My can-ti-cle di-

cries:_ May Je-sus Christ be praised! A-like at work and
find:_ May Je-sus Christ be praised! Or fades my earth-ly
this,_ May Je-sus Christ be praised! The pow'rs of dark-ness
vine,- May Je-sus Christ be praised! Be this th'e-ter-nal

pray'r To Je-sus I re-pair: May Je-sus Christ be praised!
bliss, My com-fort still is this: May Je-sus Christ be praised!
fear, When this sweet chant they hear: May Je-sus Christ be praised!
song, Through all the ag-es long. May Je-sus Christ be praised!

219 *Softly Now the Light of Day*

George W. Doane | Carl M. Von Weber

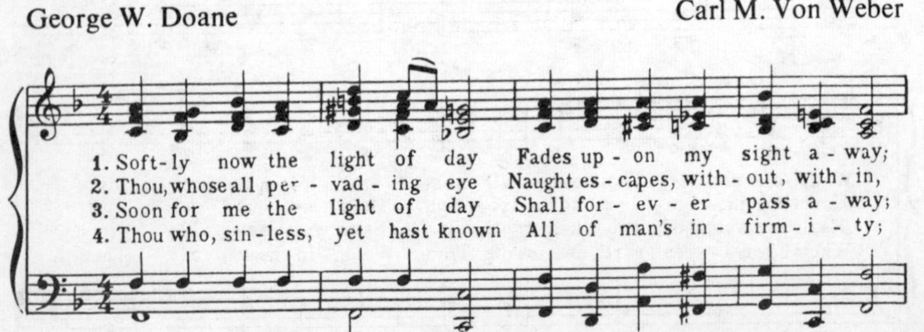
1. Soft-ly now the light of day Fades up-on my sight a-way;
2. Thou, whose all per-vad-ing eye Naught es-capes, with-out, with-in,
3. Soon for me the light of day Shall for-ev-er pass a-way;
4. Thou who, sin-less, yet hast known All of man's in-firm-i-ty;

Free from care, from la - bor_ free, Lord, I would com - mune with Thee.
Par - don each in - firm - i - ty, O - pen fault, and se - cret sin.
Then from sin and sor - row free, Take me, Lord, to_ dwell with Thee.
Then from Thine e - ter - nal throne, Je - sus, look with pity - ing eye.

220 *Jesus Loves Me, This I Know*

Anna B. Warner — William B. Bradbury

1. Je - sus loves me! this I know, For the Bi - ble tells me so;
Lit - tle ones to Him be - long; They are weak, but He is strong.

2. Je - sus loves me! He who died, Heav - en's gate to o - pen wide;
He will wash a - way my sin, Let His lit - tle child come in.

3. Je - sus loves me! loves me still, Though I'm ver - y weak and ill;
From His shin - ing throne on high, Comes to watch me where I lie.

4. Je - sus loves me! He will stay Close be - side me all the way;
If I love Him, when I die He will take me home on high.

Chorus

Yes, Je - sus loves me, Yes, Je - sus loves me,
Yes Je - sus loves me The Bi - ble tells me so.

221 Spirit Creator

From the Latin

Rev. J.A. Walsh

1. Spi - rit Cre - a - tor of man-kind
Come vis - it ev - 'ry pi - ous mind,
And sweet-ly let thy grace in - vade,
Our hearts O Lord which thou hast made.

222 *God Bless Our Native Land*

Lowell Mason (1852)

mf
1. God bless our na - tive land, Firm may she ev - er stand
2. For her our prayers shall rise To God a - bove the skies;
3. Not for this land a - lone, But be God's mer - cies known
mf

Through storm and night. When the wild tem - pests rave, Rul - er of
On Him we wait; Thou who art ev - er nigh, Guard - ing with
From shore to shore; And may the na - tions see That men should

f

wind and wave, Do Thou our coun - try save By Thy great_ might.
watch - ful eye, To Thee a - loud we cry, God save the___ state.
broth - ers be, And form one fam - i - ly The wide world_ o'er.

f

223 *Song in the Fields*

Marian Singers

Refrain:

A D
There's song in the fields and song in the flowers,

A E7 A
Joy in my heart all day. There's song in the fields and

D A E7 A
song in the flowers, Joy in the Lord who lights my way.

Verse:

A
All the ways of this world lead you With the

E7 A
joys of friend-ship strewn, To your brother who may

D A E7 A
need you And who hopes to meet you soon.

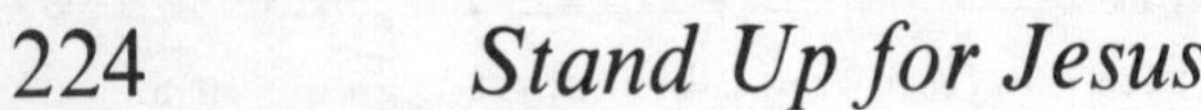

224 *Stand Up for Jesus*

George Duffield George J. Webb

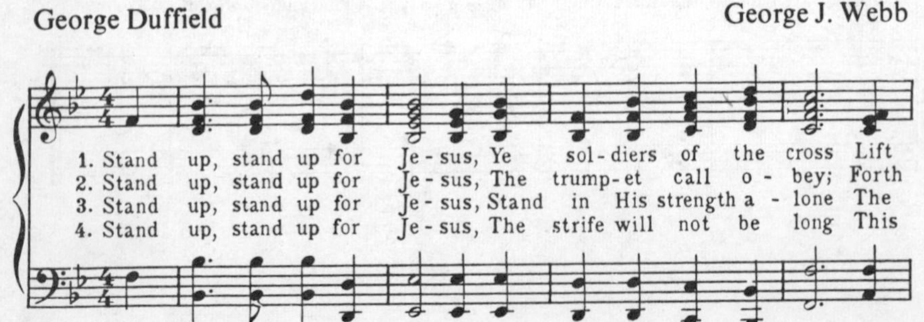
1. Stand up, stand up for Je - sus, Ye sol - diers of the cross Lift
2. Stand up, stand up for Je - sus, The trump - et call o - bey; Forth
3. Stand up, stand up for Je - sus, Stand in His strength a - lone The
4. Stand up, stand up for Je - sus, The strife will not be long This

high His roy - al ban - ner It must not suf - fer loss; From
to the might - y con - flict, In this His glo - rious day. "Ye
arm of flesh will fail you Ye dare not trust your own; Put
day the noise of bat - tle, The next, the vic - tor's song; To
vic - t'ry un - to vic - t'ry, His ar - my shall He lead,— Till
that are men, now serve Him," A - gainst un - num - bered foes;— Let
on the gos - pel ar - mor, Each piece put on with pray'r; Where
him that o - ver - com - eth, A crown of life shall be;— He
ev - 'ry foe is van - quished And Christ is Lord in - deed.
cour - age rise with dan - ger, And strength to strength op - pose.
du - ty calls, or dan - ger, Be nev - er want - ing there.
with the King of glo - ry Shall reign e - ter - nal - ly.
mf
1. Glo - ry be to God, the Fa - ther, Glo - ry be — to God, — the Son.
2. Glo - ry to the King of an - gels, Glo - ry to — the Church's King.
mf
cresc.
dim.
Glo - ry be to God, the Spir - it, Great — Je - ho - vah, Three in One.
Glo - ry to the King of Na - tions, Heav'n — and earth your prais - es bring.
cresc.
dim.

225 *The Holy Trinity*

Rev. Horatio Bonar — W. A. Mozart

Glo-ry be to Him who loved us, To the Lamb that once was slain. Glo-ry be to
Glo-ry, bless-ing, praise e-ter-nal! Thus the choir of an-gels sing. Hon-or, rich-es,
1.
2. cresc.
rit.
Him who bought us, Made us kings with Him to reign.
pow'r, do-min-ion! Thus its praise cre-a-tion brings.
cresc.
rit.

226 *Hark! Hark! My Soul*

Father Faber

Henry Smart

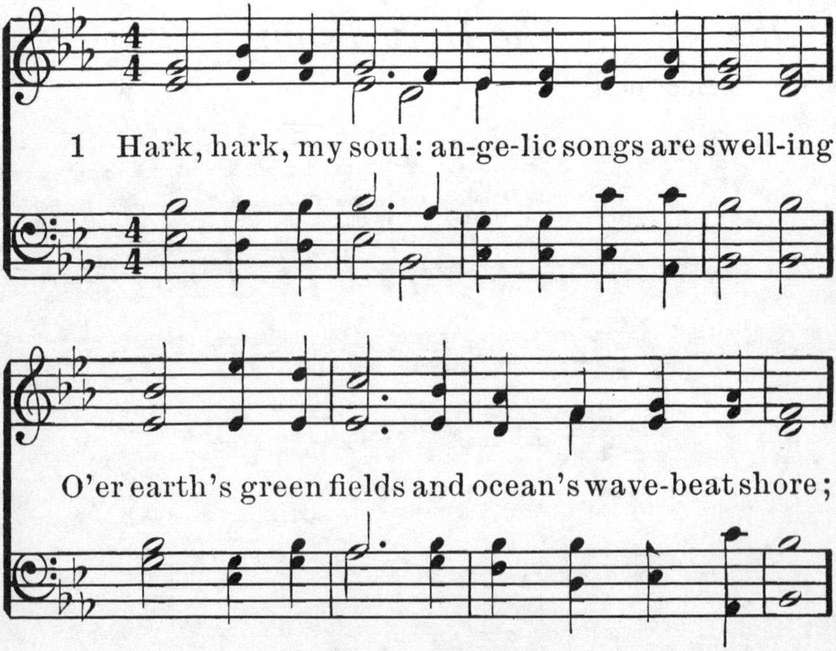

1 Hark, hark, my soul: an-ge-lic songs are swell-ing

O'er earth's green fields and ocean's wave-beat shore;

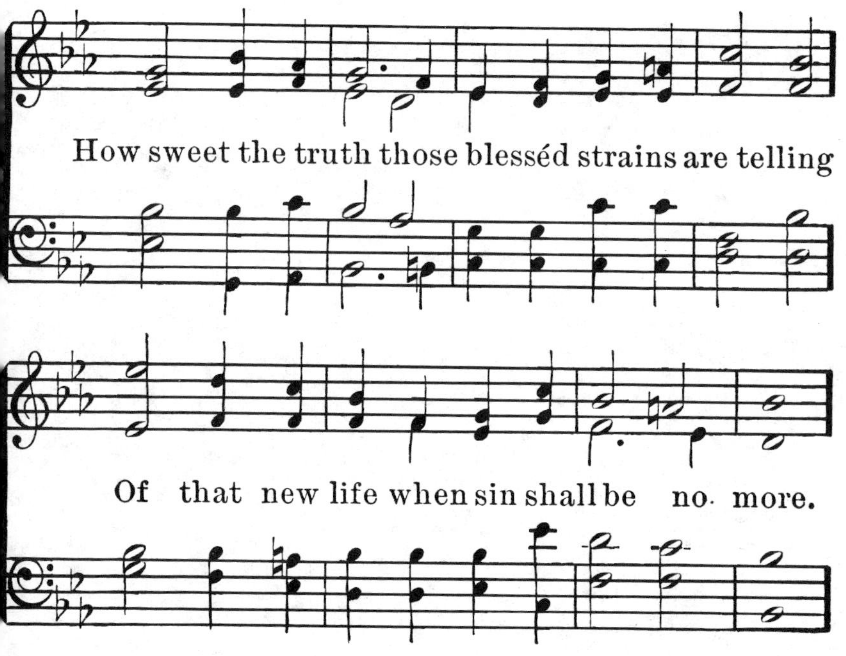
How sweet the truth those blesséd strains are telling
Of that new life when sin shall be no more.

2. Rest comes at length; though life be long and dreary
The day must dawn, and darksome night be past:
All journeys end in welcomes to the weary,
All heaven, the heart's true home, will come at last.

LATIN MASSES

XI *Orbis Factor*

VIII *De Angelis*

XI Orbis Factor

Harmonized by Achille P. Bragers

227 *Kyrie*

Ký-ri-e * e - - lé-i-son.iij.Chrí-ste
e - - lé-i-son.iij. Ký-ri-e e - - lé-i-son.ij.
Ký - ri - e * e - - lé - i - son.
228
Gloria
Gló-ri-a in ex-cél-sis Dé-o. Et in tér-ra pax ho-mí-ni-
bus bó-nae vo-lun-tá-tis. Lau-dá-mus te. Be-ne-dí-ci-mus te.

Ad-o-rá-mus te. Glo-ri-fi-cá-mus te. Grá-ti-as á-gi-mus tí-bi
pró-pter má-gnam gló-ri-am tú-am. Dó-mi-ne Dé-us, Rex cae-lé-stis,
Dé-us Pá-ter o-mní-po-tens. Dó-mi-ne Fí-li u-ni-gé-ni-te,
Jé-su Chrí-ste. Dó-mi-ne Dé-us, A-gnus Dé-i, Fí-li-us Pá-tris.
Qui tól-lis pec-cá-ta mún-di, mi-se-ré-re nó-bis. Qui tól-lis pec-cá-ta

mún - di, sús - ci - pe de - pre - ca - ti - ó - nem nó - stram. Qui sé - des ad
déx - te - ram Pá - tris, mi - se - ré - re nó - bis. Quó - ni - am
tu só - lus sán - ctus. Tu só - lus Dó - mi - nus. Tu só - lus Al - tís - si - mus,
Jé - su Chrí - ste. Cum Sán - cto Spí - ri - tu in gló - ri - a
Dé - i Pá - tris. A - men.

229 *Credo III*

Cré-do in ú-num Dé - um, Pá-trem o-mni-po-tén-tem, fa-ctó-rem coé-li et
tér-rae, vi-si-bí-li-um ó - mní-um, et in-vi-si-bí · · li-um. Et in ú-num Dó-mi-
num Jé-sum Chrí-stum, Fí-li-um Dé-i u-ni-gé-ni-tum. Et ex Pá-tre ná - tum
an-te ó-mni-a saé - cu-la. Dé-um de Dé-o, lú-men dé lú-mi-ne, Dé-um vé-rum
de Dé-o vé - ro. Gé-ni-tum, non fá - ctum, con-sub-stan-ti-á-lem Pá-tri, per quem

ó-mni-a fá-cta sunt. Qui próp-ter nos hó-mi-nes, et prop-ter nó-stram sa-lú-tem descéndit
de coé-lis. Et in-car-ná-tus est de Spí-ri-tu Sán-cto ex Má-ri - a Vír-gi - ne:
Et hó-mo fá-ctus est. Cru-cí - fi - xus é-ti-am pro nó-bis: sub Pon-tí-o Pi-lá - to
pás-sus, et se-púl - tus est. Et re-sur-ré-xit ter-tí - a dí - e se-cúndum Scriptú-ras.
Et a-scén-dit in coé - lum sé-det ad déx-te-ram Pá - tris. Et í - te-rum ven-tú-rus
est cum gló-ri - a, ju-di-cá-re ví-vos et mór-tu-os: cú-jus ré-gni non é-rit fí - nis.

Et in Spí-ri-tum San-ctum Dó-mi-num, et vi-vi-fi-cán-tem: qui ex Pá-tre Fi-li-o-
que pro-cé-dit. Qui cum Pá-tre et Fí-li-o si-mul a-do-rá-tur, et con-glo-
ri-fi-cá-tur: qui lo-cú-tus est per Pro-phé-tas. Et ú-nam sán-ctam ca-thó-li-cam
et a-po-stó-li-cam Ec-clé-si-am. Con-fí-te-or ú-num bap-tí-sma
in re-mis-si-ó-nem pec-ca-tó-rum. Et ex-spé-cto re-sur-re-cti-ó-nem mor-tu-ó-rum.
Et vi-tam ven-tú-ri sae-cu-li. A - - - - - - men.

Sanctus

Sán - ctus,* Sán - ctus, Sán - ctus Dó - mi - nus
Dé - us Sá - ba - oth. Plé - ni - sunt cáe - li et ter - ra
gló - ri - a tú - a. Ho - sán - na in ex - cél - sis.
Be - ne - dí - ctus qui vé - nit in nó - mi - ne Dó - mi -
ni. Hó - san - na in ex - cél - sis.

231 *Agnus Dei*

A - gnus Dé - i ∗ qui tól - lis pec - cá - ta mún - di:

mi - se - ré - re nó - bis. A - gnus Dé - i ∗ qui tól - lis pec - cá - ta

mún - di: mi - se - ré - re nó - bis. A - gnus Dé - i ∗ qui

tól - lis pec - cá - ta mún - di; dó - na nó - bis pá - cem.

232 *Deo Gratias*

Dé - o grá - - ti - as.

VIII De Angelis

233 *Kyrie*

Harmonized by Achille P. Bragers

Ký - ri - e * e - -
- lé - i - son. iij. Chrí - ste
e - - lé - i - son. iij. Ký - ri - e
e - - lé - i - son. ij. Ký - ri - e *
** e - - lé - i - son.

234

Gloria

Gló-ri-a in ex-cél-sis Dé - o. Et in tér-ra pax ho-mí-ni-bus bó-nae
vo-lun-tá-tis. Lau-dá - mus te. Be-ne-dí-ci-mus te. Ad-o-rá -
mus te. Glo-ri-fi-cá-mus te. Grá-ti-as á-gi-mus tí-bi pró-pter má-gnam
gló-ri-am tú - am. Dó-mi-ne Dé-us, Rex cæ-lé-stis, Dé-us Pá-ter o -
mní-po-tens. Dó-mi-ne Fí-li u-ni-gé-ni-te Jé-su Chrí-ste.

Dó-mi-ne Dé-us. A-gnus Dé-i, Fí-li-us Pá-tris. Qui tól-lis pec-cá-ta
mún-di mi-se-ré-re nó-bis. Qui tól-lis pec-cá-ta mún-di,
sú-sci-pe de-pre-ca-ti-ó-nem nó-stram. Qui sé-des ad déx-te-ram Pá-tris,
mi-se-ré-re nó-bis. Quó-ni-am tu só-lus sán-ctus. Tu só-lus Dó-mi-nus.
Tu só-lus Al-tís-si-mus, Jé-su Chri-ste. Cum Sán-cto
Spí-ri-tu in gló-ri-a Dé-i Pá-tris. A-men.
Ped.

235 Sanctus

Sán - ctus,*Sán-ctus, San - ctus Dó - mi-nus
Dé-us Sá - - - ba-oth. Plé-ni-sunt cae-li
et tér - ra gló-ri-a tú - a. Ho-sán-na in ex-cél-
- - sis. Be-ne-dí - ctus qui vé - nit in nó-mi-ne Dó -
mi-ni. Ho-sán - - na in ex-cél - - sis.

236 *Agnus Dei*

A - gnus Dé - i, * qui tól - lis pec - cá - ta mún - di:

mi - se - ré - re nó - bis. A - gnus Dé - i, * qui tól - lis

pec - cá - ta mún - di: mi - se - ré - re nó - bis. A - gnus

Dé - i, * qui tól - lis pec - cá - ta mún - di: dó - na nó - bis pá - cem.

237 *Deo Gratias*

Dé - o ________ grá - ti - as.